GREATEST SPORTS

A WIN FOR WOMEN

BILLIE JEAN KING TAKES DOWN BOBBY RIGGS

BY BRANDON TERRELL

ILLUSTRATED BY EDUARDO GARCIA AND RED WOLF STUDIO

CONSULTANT:

BRUCE BERGLUND

PROFESSOR OF HISTORY, CALVIN COLLEGE

GRAND RAPIDS, MICHIGAN

CAPSTONE PRESS

a capstone imprint

Graphic Library is published by Capstone Press,
1710 Roe Crest Drive, North Mankato, Minnesota 56003
www.mycapstone.com

Library of Congress Cataloging-in-Publication data
Names: Terrell, Brandon, 1978– author.
Title: A win for women : Billie Jean King takes down Bobby Riggs / by Brandon Terrell.
Description: North Mankato, Minnesota : An imprint of Capstone Press, [2019] | Series: Graphic Library.
    Greatest sports moments | Audience: Ages: 8–14.
Identifiers: LCCN 2018029923 (print) | LCCN 2018042516 (ebook) | ISBN 9781543542233 (ebook PDF) |
    ISBN 9781543542196 (hardcover) | ISBN 9781543542219 (paperback)
Subjects: LCSH: King, Billie Jean—Juvenile literature. | Riggs, Bobby, 1918–1995—Juvenile literature. |
    Tennis players—United States—Biography—Juvenile literature. | Sex discrimination in sports—
    Juvenile literature. | Sports—Sex differences.
Classification: LCC GV994.K56 (ebook) | LCC GV994.K56 T47 2019 (print) | DDC 796.3420922 [B]—dc23
LC record available at https://lccn.loc.gov/2018029923

Summary: In graphic novel format, tells the story of the famous "Battle of the Sexes" tennis match between Billie Jean King and Bobby Riggs in 1973.

EDITOR
Aaron J. Sautter

ART DIRECTOR
Nathan Gassman

DESIGNER
Kyle Grenz

MEDIA RESEARCHER
Eric Gohl

PRODUCTION SPECIALIST
Katy LaVigne

Direct quotations appear in **bold italicized text** on the following pages:

Pages 6, 7: from "When Billie Beat Bobby," by Jesse Greenspan, September 20, 2013 (https://www.history.com/news/ billie-jean-king-wins-the-battle-of-the-sexes-40-years-ago).
Page 9, 14, 26, 29: from *Necessary Spectacle*, by Selena Roberts.
Page 28: from "Billie Jean King Receives Presidential Medal of Freedom," by Liz Clarke, Washington Post, August 13, 2009 (http://www.washingtonpost.com/wp-dyn/content/article/2009/08/12/AR2009081203037.html?noredirect=on).

Printed and bound in the United States of America.
022019   001628

TABLE OF CONTENTS

THE STAGE IS SET

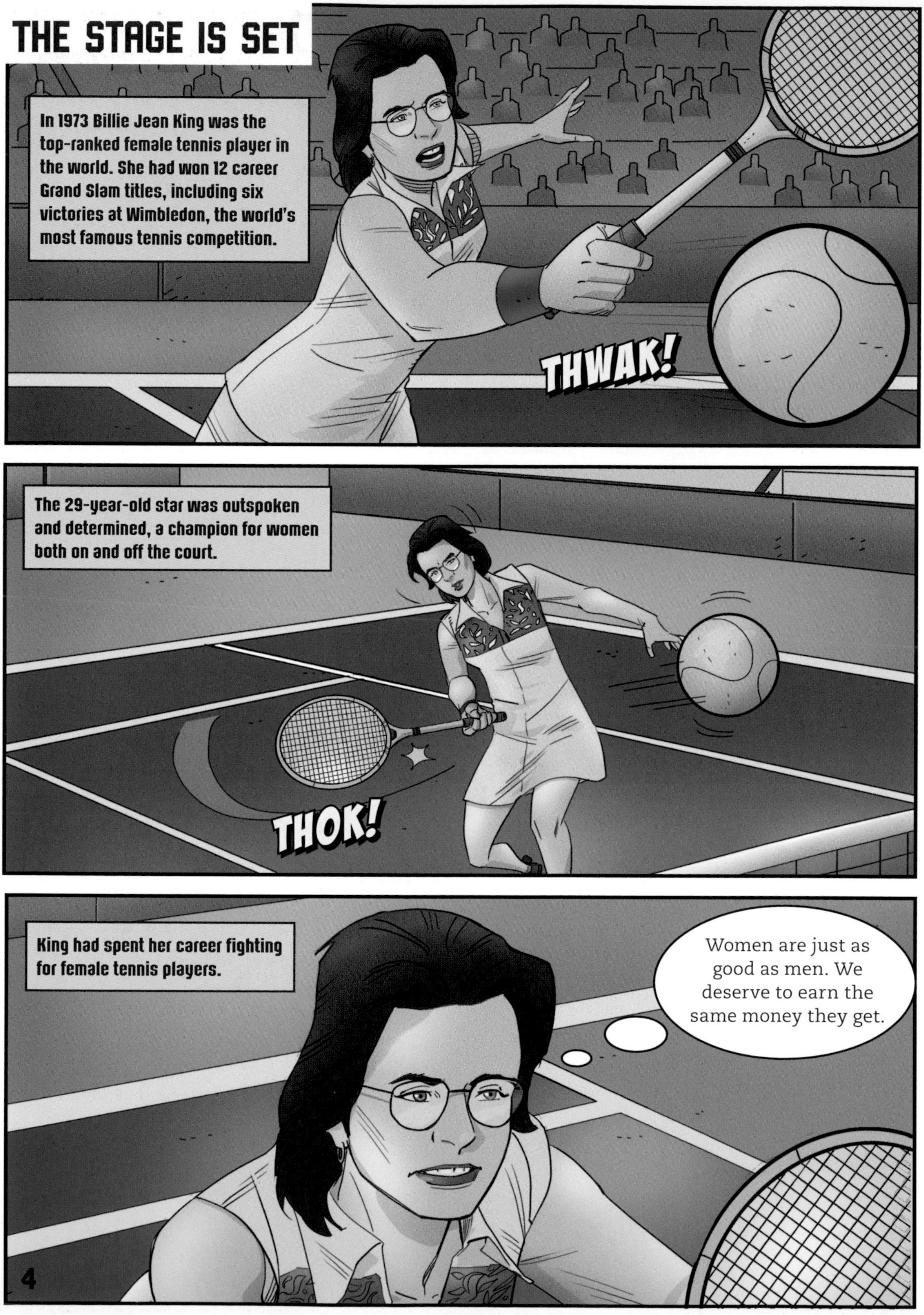
In 1973 Billie Jean King was the top-ranked female tennis player in the world. She had won 12 career Grand Slam titles, including six victories at Wimbledon, the world's most famous tennis competition.
THWAK!
The 29-year-old star was outspoken and determined, a champion for women both on and off the court.
THOK!
King had spent her career fighting for female tennis players.
Women are just as good as men. We deserve to earn the same money they get.

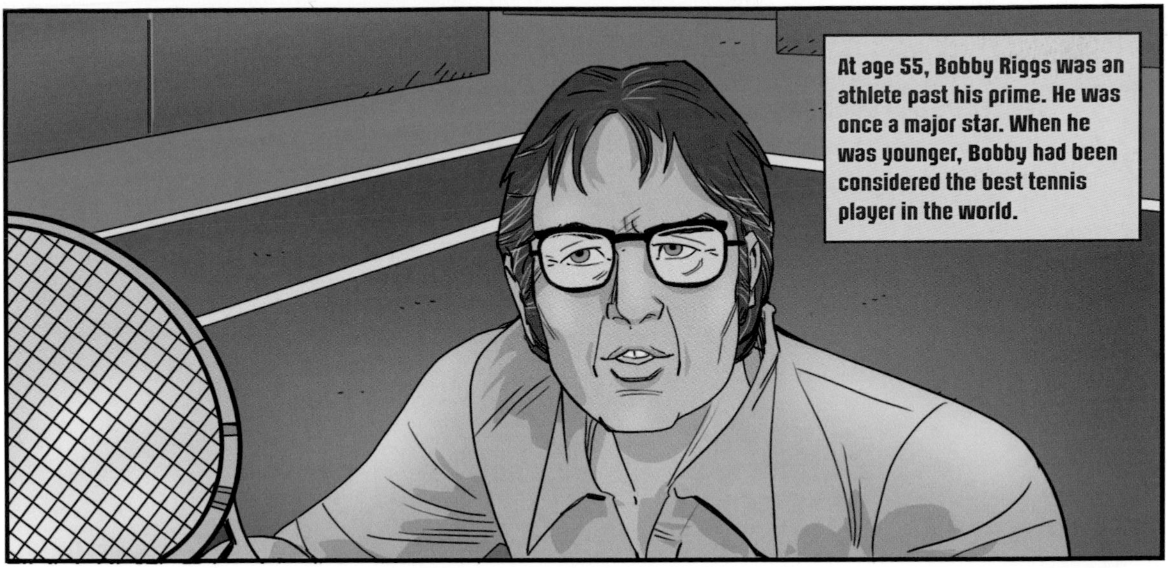
At age 55, Bobby Riggs was an athlete past his prime. He was once a major star. When he was younger, Bobby had been considered the best tennis player in the world.

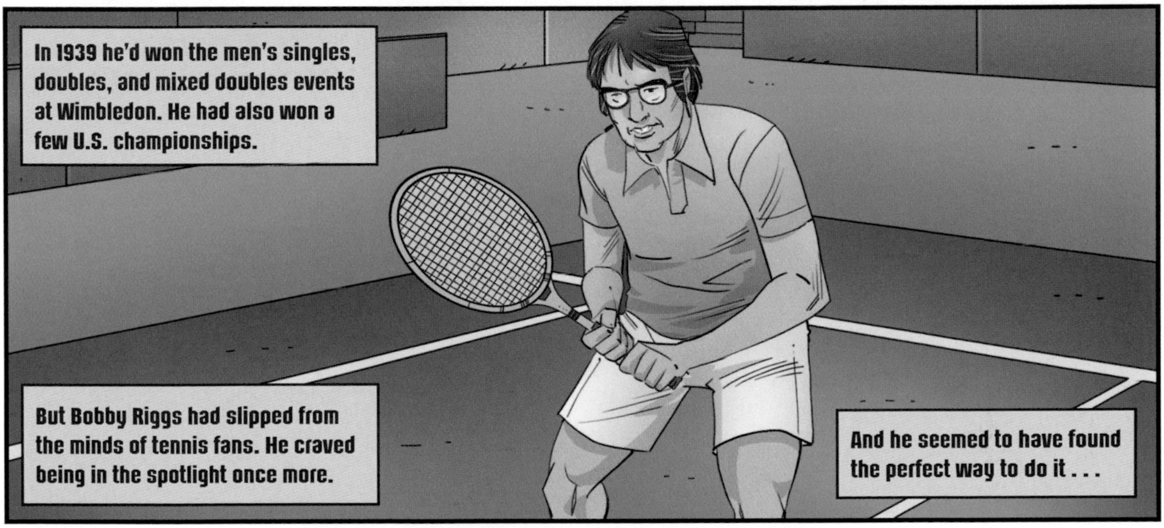
In 1939 he'd won the men's singles, doubles, and mixed doubles events at Wimbledon. He had also won a few U.S. championships.
But Bobby Riggs had slipped from the minds of tennis fans. He craved being in the spotlight once more.
And he seemed to have found the perfect way to do it . . .

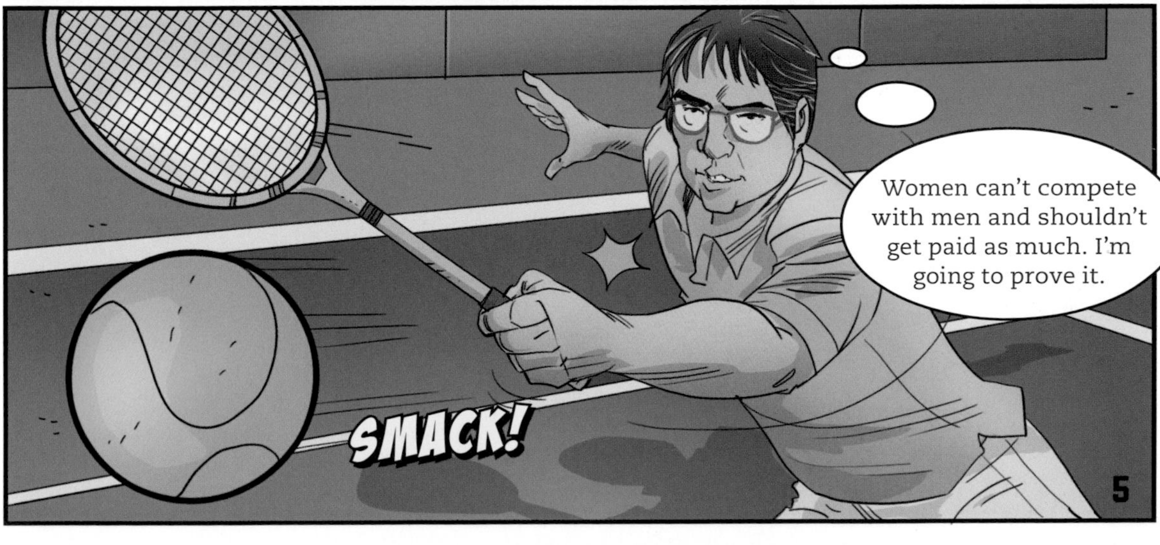
Women can't compete with men and shouldn't get paid as much. I'm going to prove it.
SMACK!

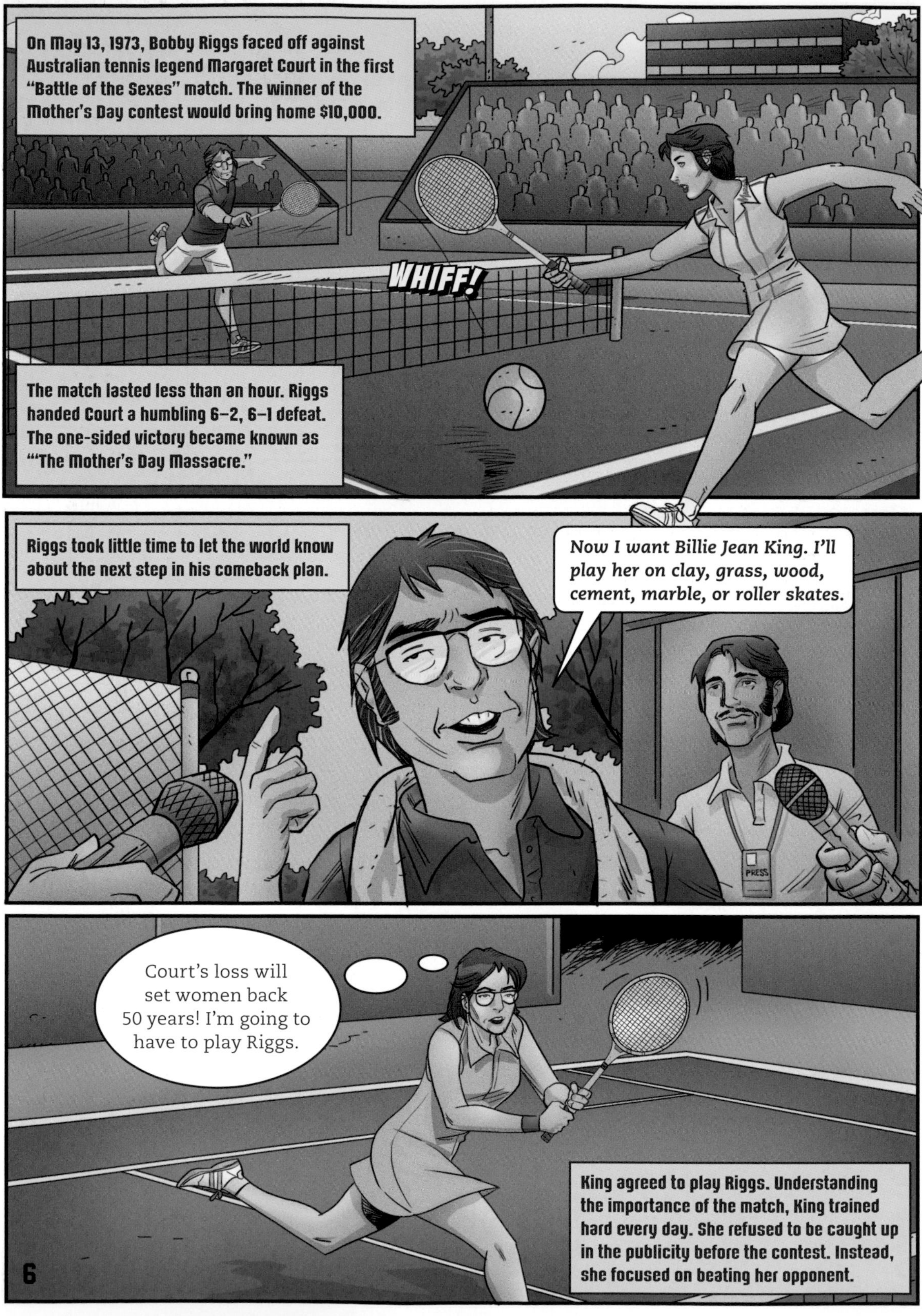
On May 13, 1973, Bobby Riggs faced off against Australian tennis legend Margaret Court in the first "Battle of the Sexes" match. The winner of the Mother's Day contest would bring home $10,000.
WHIFF!
The match lasted less than an hour. Riggs handed Court a humbling 6–2, 6–1 defeat. The one-sided victory became known as "'The Mother's Day Massacre."
Riggs took little time to let the world know about the next step in his comeback plan.
Now I want Billie Jean King. I'll play her on clay, grass, wood, cement, marble, or roller skates.
PRESS
Court's loss will set women back 50 years! I'm going to have to play Riggs.
King agreed to play Riggs. Understanding the importance of the match, King trained hard every day. She refused to be caught up in the publicity before the contest. Instead, she focused on beating her opponent.

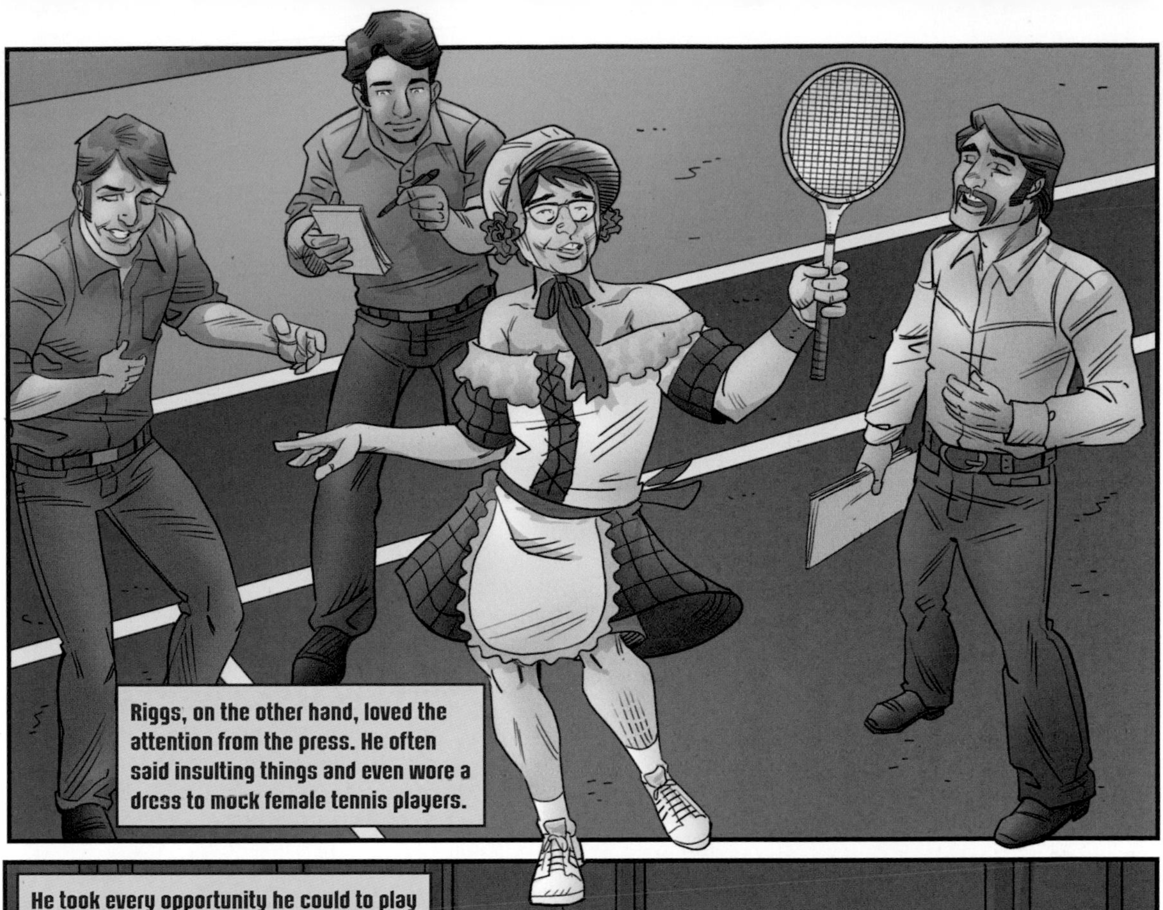
Riggs, on the other hand, loved the attention from the press. He often said insulting things and even wore a dress to mock female tennis players.

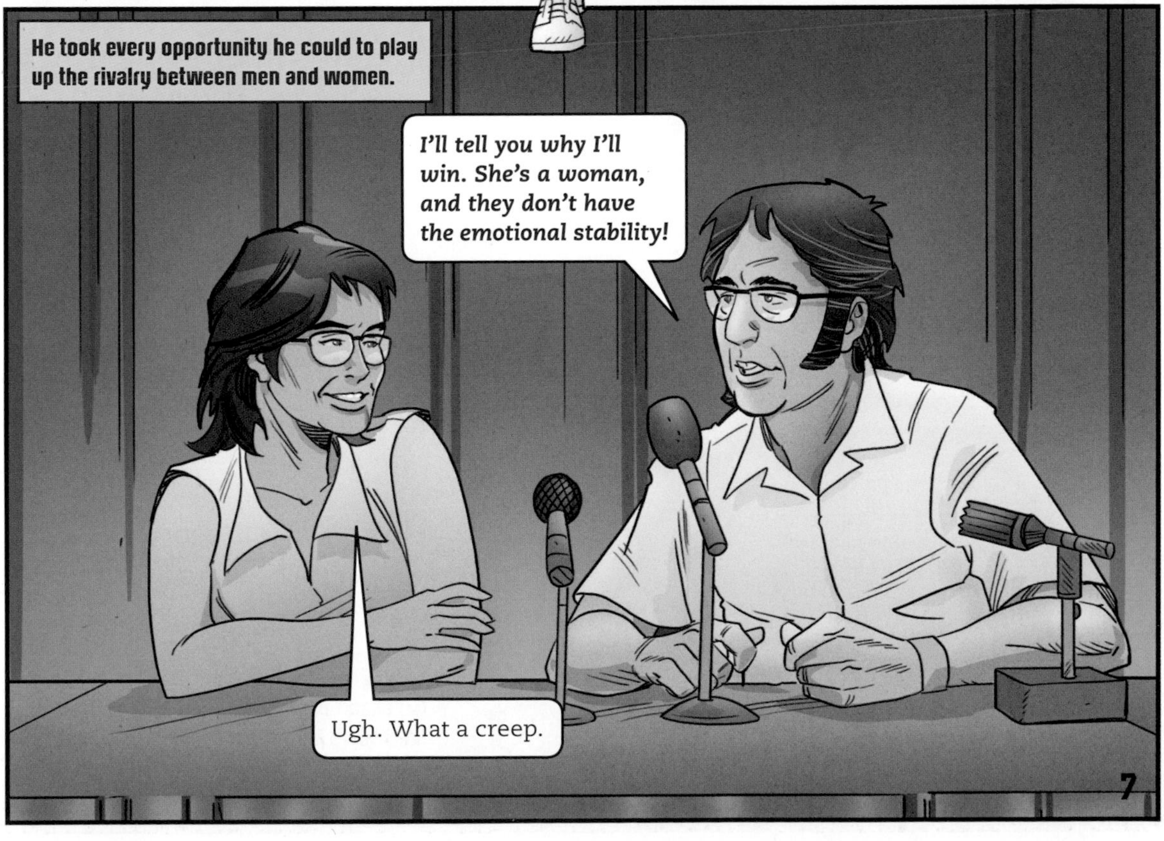
He took every opportunity he could to play up the rivalry between men and women.
I'll tell you why I'll win. She's a woman, and they don't have the emotional stability!
Ugh. What a creep.

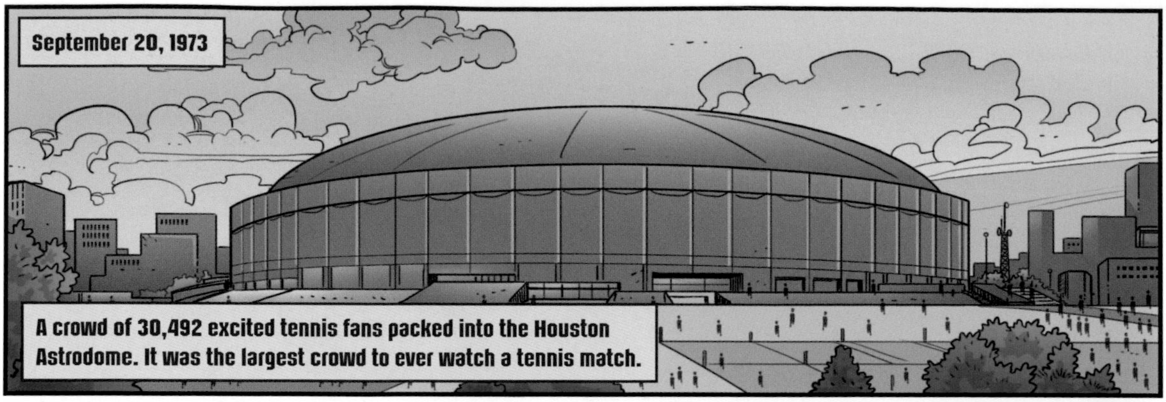
September 20, 1973
A crowd of 30,492 excited tennis fans packed into the Houston Astrodome. It was the largest crowd to ever watch a tennis match.

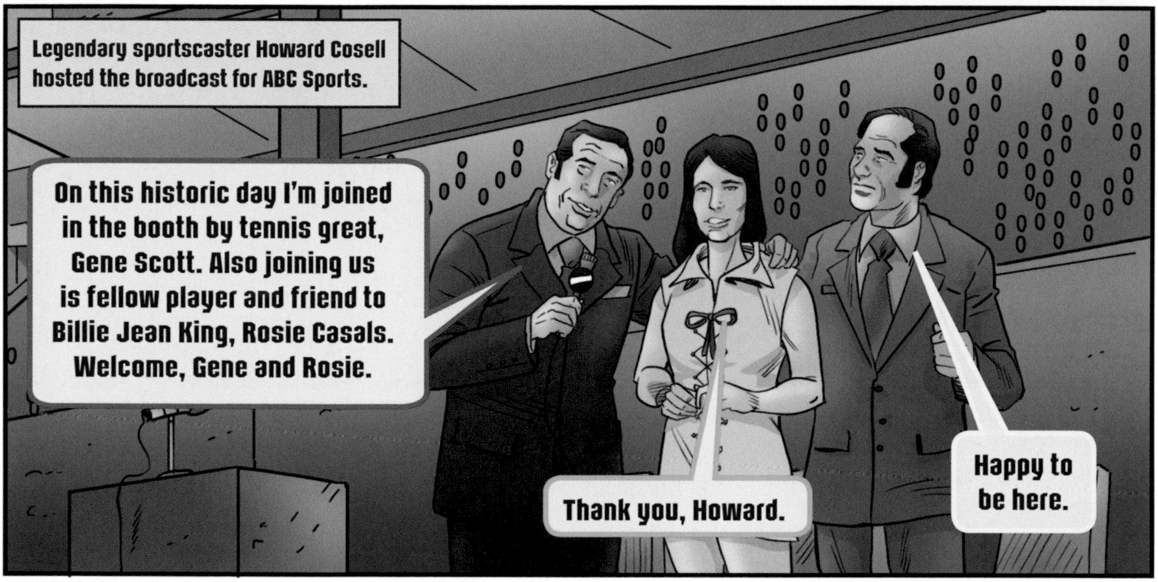
Legendary sportscaster Howard Cosell hosted the broadcast for ABC Sports.
On this historic day I'm joined in the booth by tennis great, Gene Scott. Also joining us is fellow player and friend to Billie Jean King, Rosie Casals. Welcome, Gene and Rosie.
Thank you, Howard.
Happy to be here.

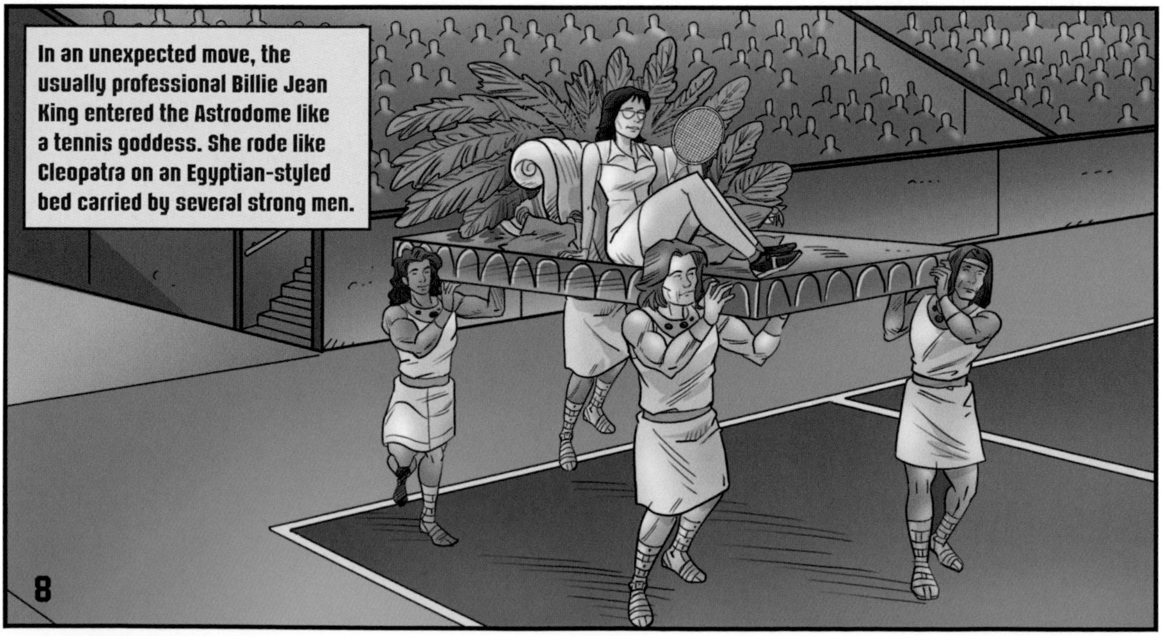
In an unexpected move, the usually professional Billie Jean King entered the Astrodome like a tennis goddess. She rode like Cleopatra on an Egyptian-styled bed carried by several strong men.

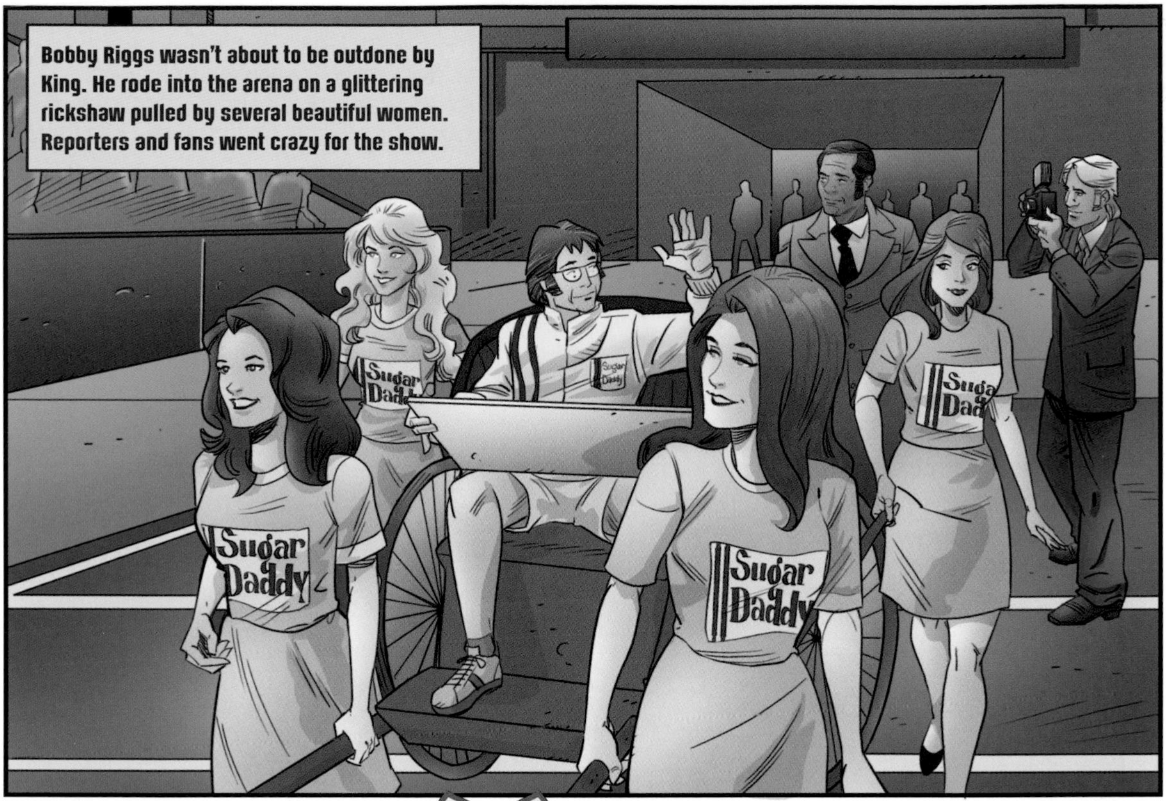

Bobby Riggs wasn't about to be outdone by King. He rode into the arena on a glittering rickshaw pulled by several beautiful women. Reporters and fans went crazy for the show.
Sugar Daddy

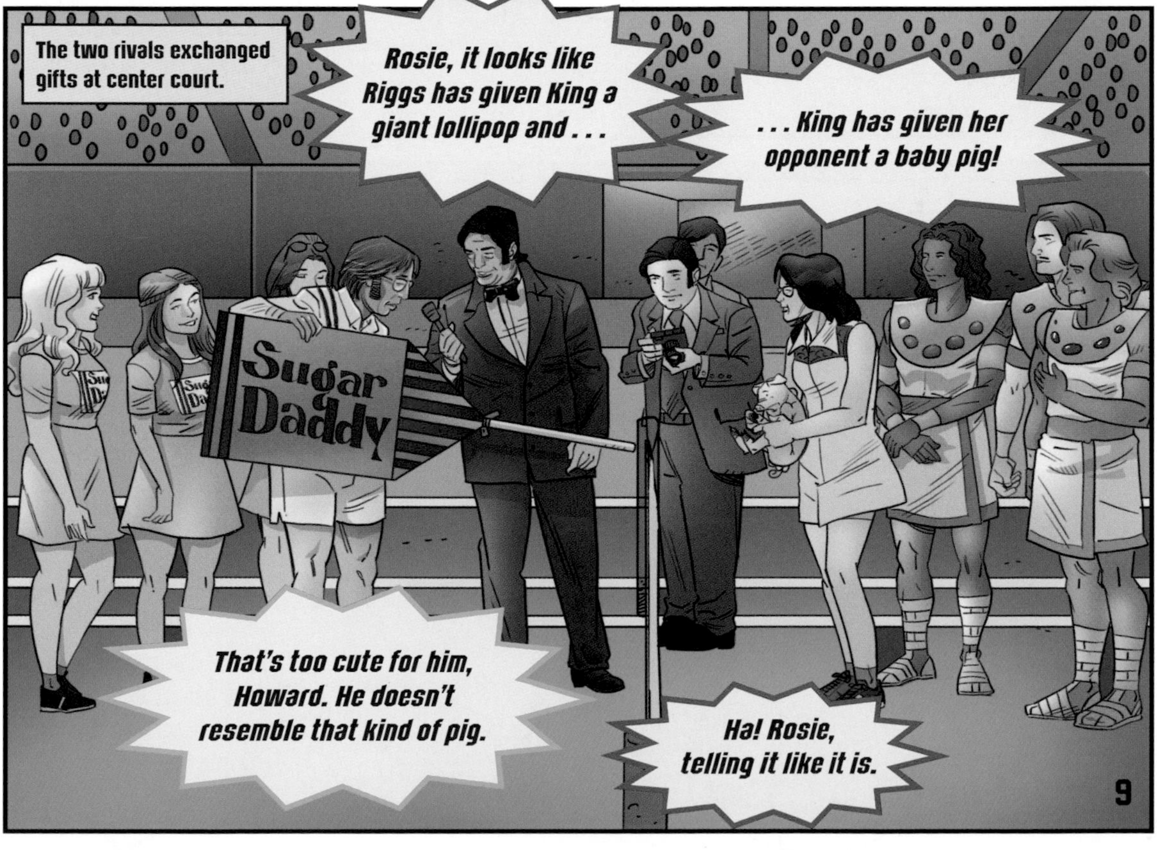

The two rivals exchanged gifts at center court.
Rosie, it looks like Riggs has given King a giant lollipop and . . .
. . . King has given her opponent a baby pig!
Sugar Daddy
That's too cute for him, Howard. He doesn't resemble that kind of pig.
Ha! Rosie, telling it like it is.

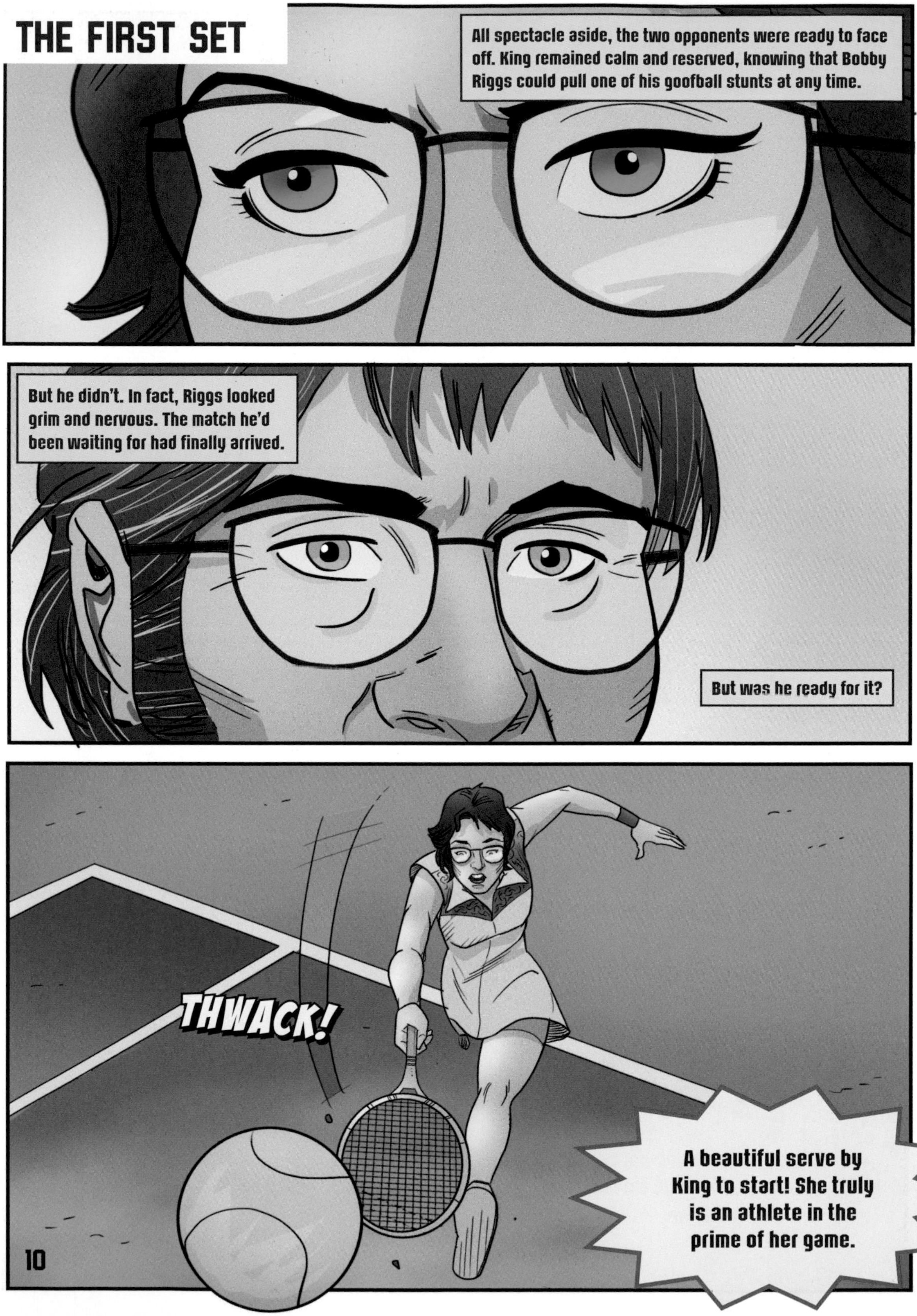
THE FIRST SET
All spectacle aside, the two opponents were ready to face off. King remained calm and reserved, knowing that Bobby Riggs could pull one of his goofball stunts at any time.
But he didn't. In fact, Riggs looked grim and nervous. The match he'd been waiting for had finally arrived.
But was he ready for it?
THWACK!
A beautiful serve by King to start! She truly is an athlete in the prime of her game.

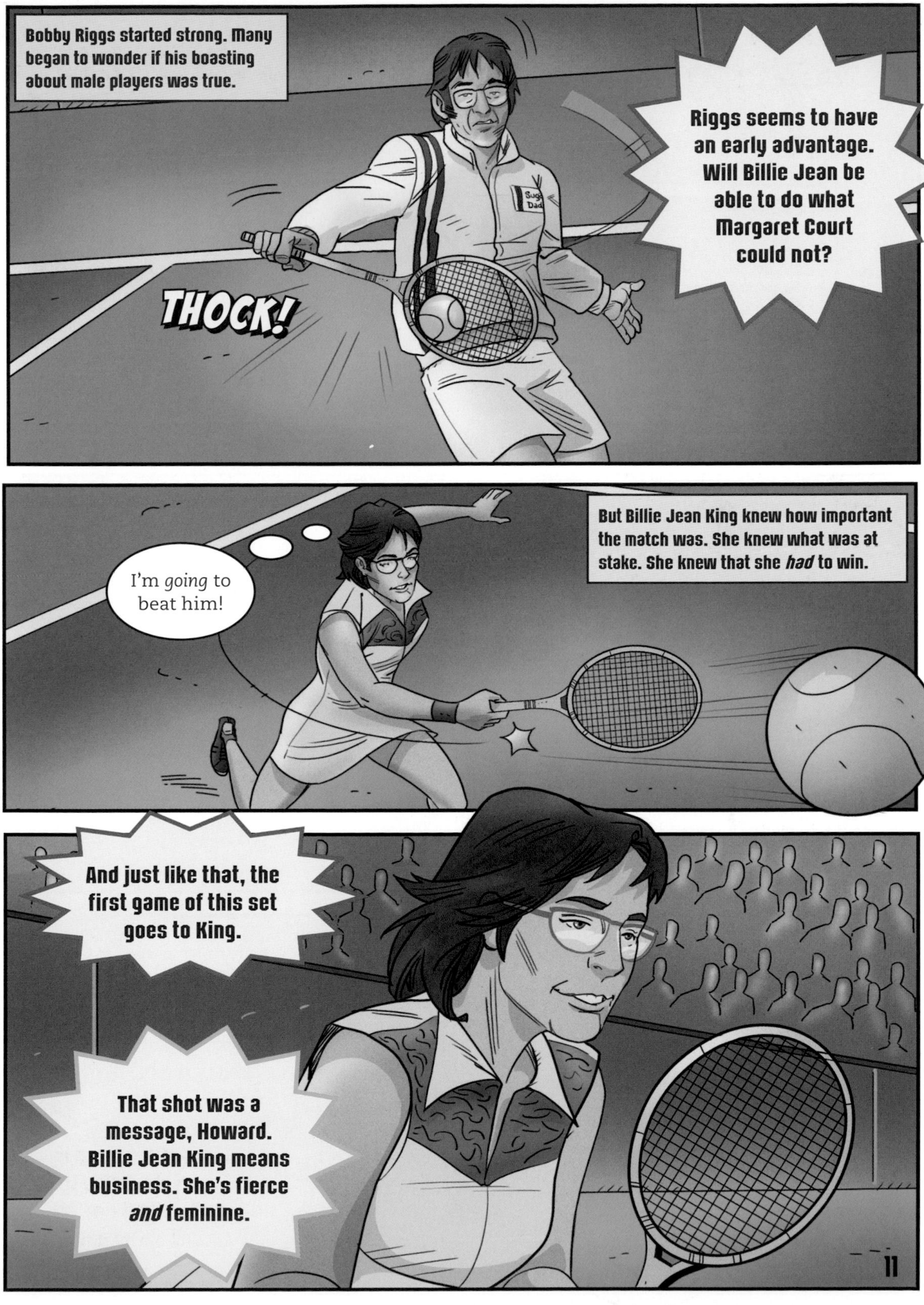
Bobby Riggs started strong. Many began to wonder if his boasting about male players was true.
Riggs seems to have an early advantage. Will Billie Jean be able to do what Margaret Court could not?
THOCK!
I'm *going* to beat him!
But Billie Jean King knew how important the match was. She knew what was at stake. She knew that she *had* to win.
And just like that, the first game of this set goes to King.
That shot was a message, Howard. Billie Jean King means business. She's fierce *and* feminine.

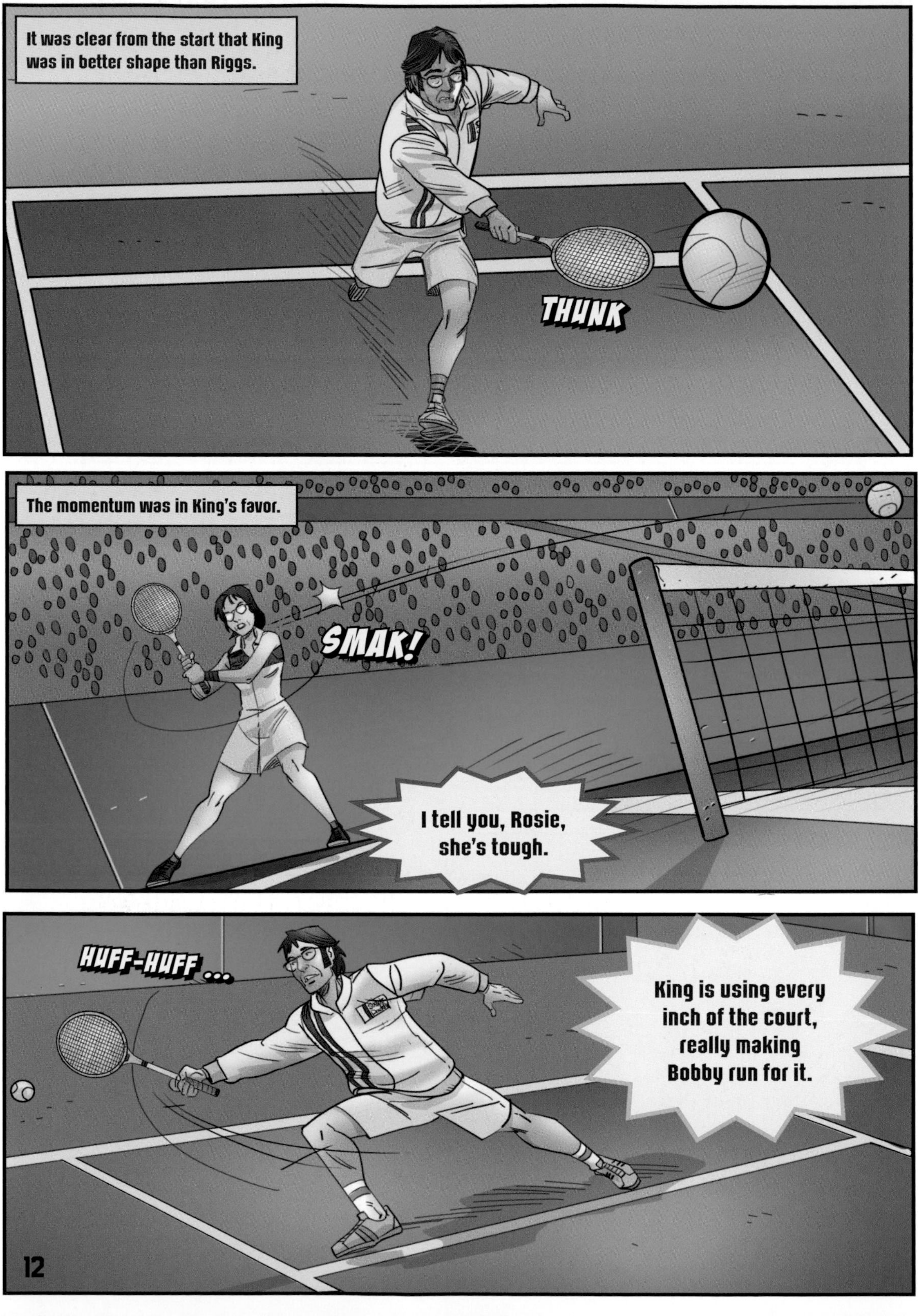
It was clear from the start that King was in better shape than Riggs.
THUNK
The momentum was in King's favor.
SMAK!
I tell you, Rosie, she's tough.
HUFF-HUFF ...
King is using every inch of the court, really making Bobby run for it.

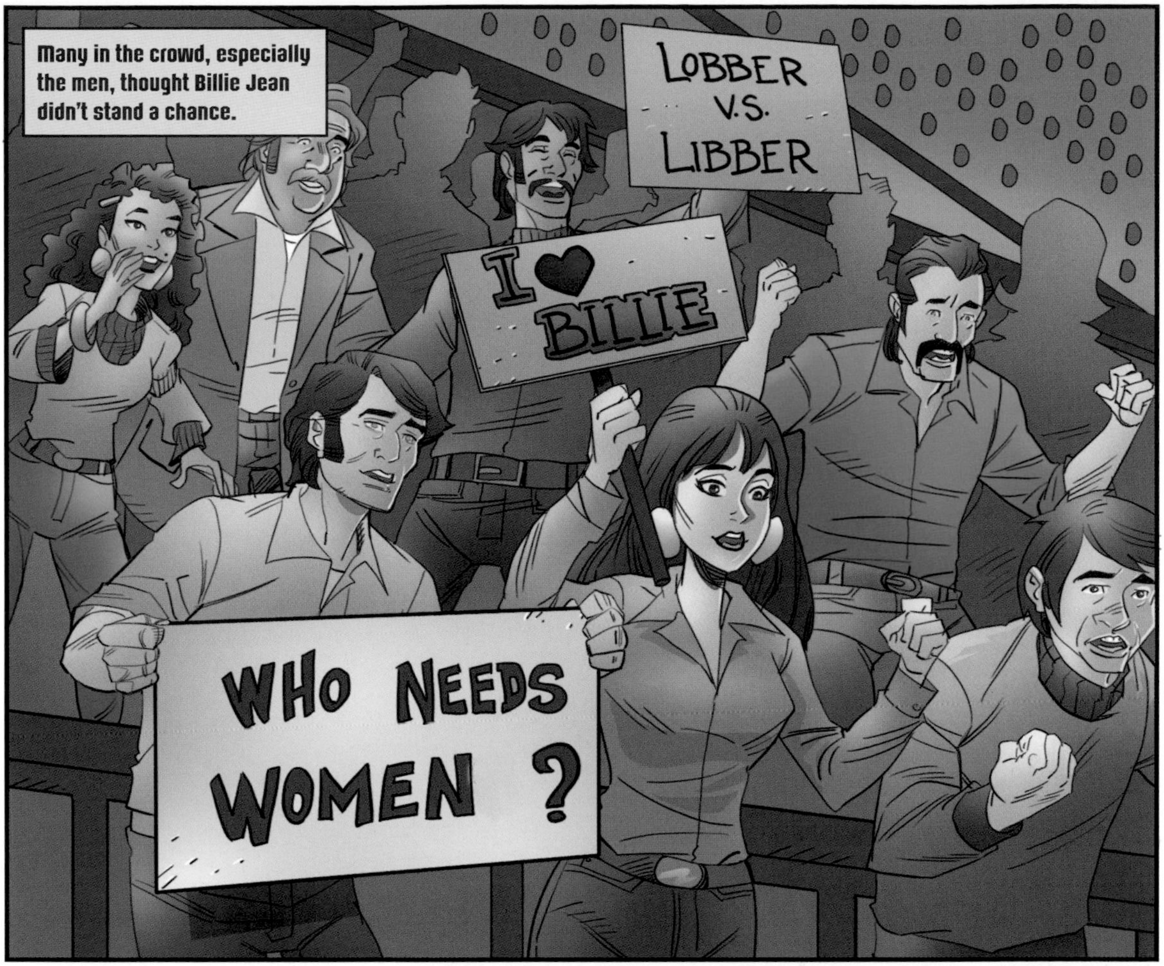
Many in the crowd, especially the men, thought Billie Jean didn't stand a chance.
LOBBER V.S. LIBBER
I ♥ BILLIE
WHO NEEDS WOMEN ?

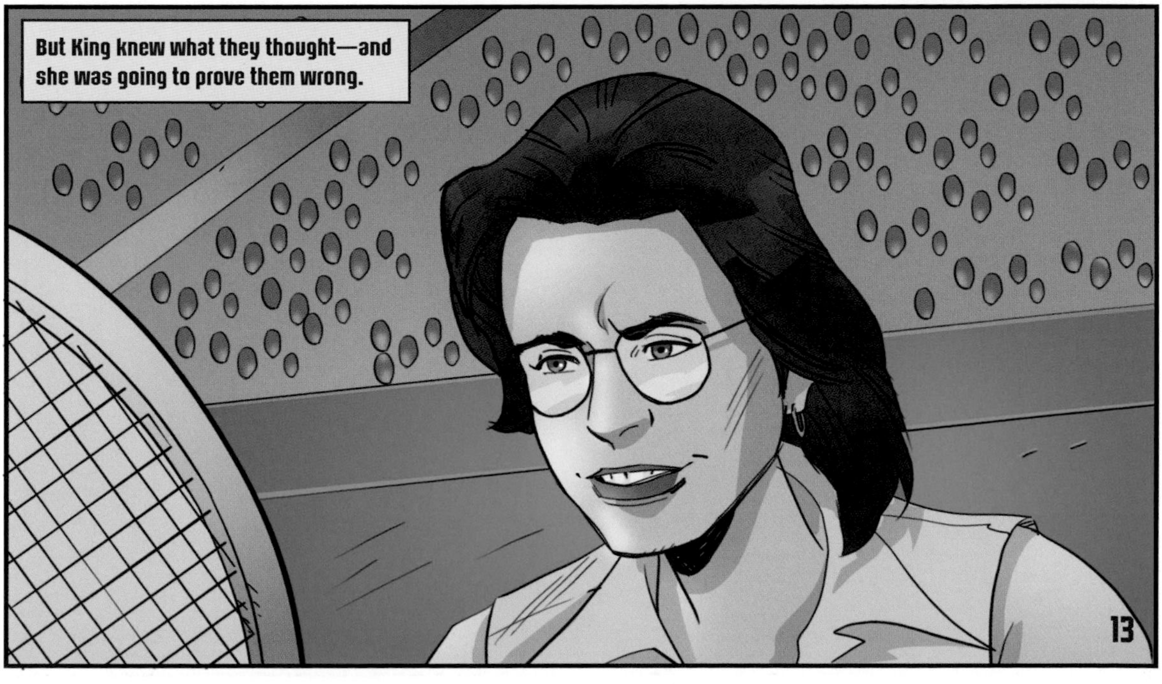
But King knew what they thought—and she was going to prove them wrong.

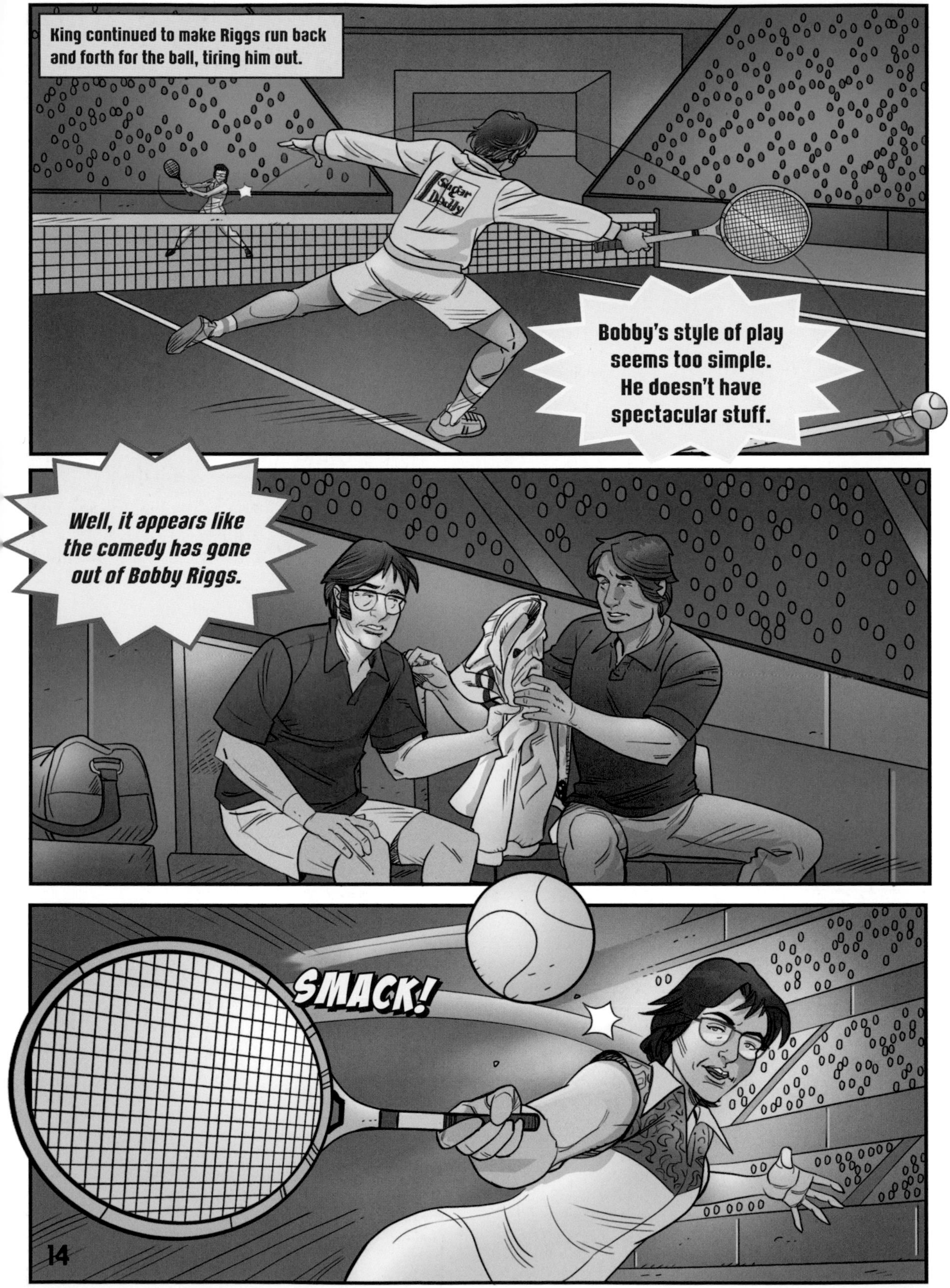
King continued to make Riggs run back and forth for the ball, tiring him out.
Sugar Daddy
Bobby's style of play seems too simple. He doesn't have spectacular stuff.
Well, it appears like the comedy has gone out of Bobby Riggs.
SMACK!

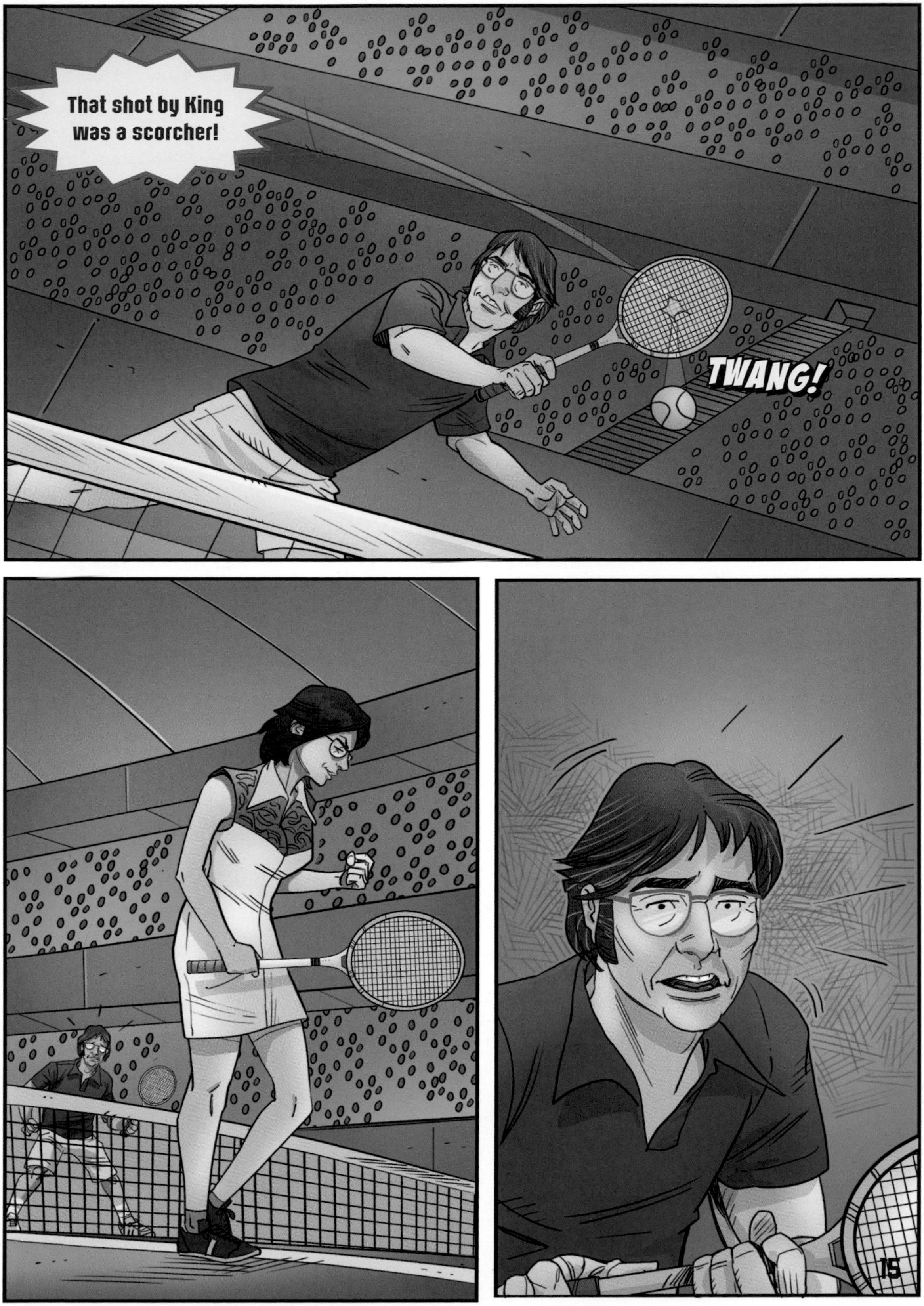
That shot by King was a scorcher!
TWANG!

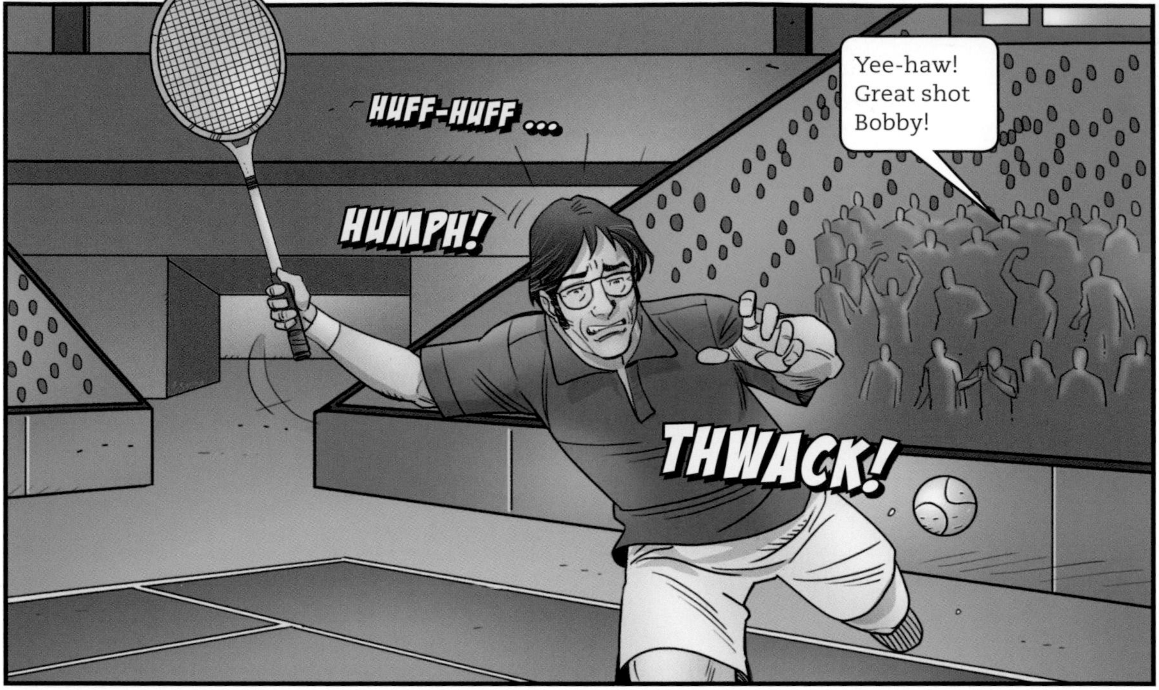
HUFF-HUFF ...
HUMPH!
Yee-haw! Great shot Bobby!
THWACK!

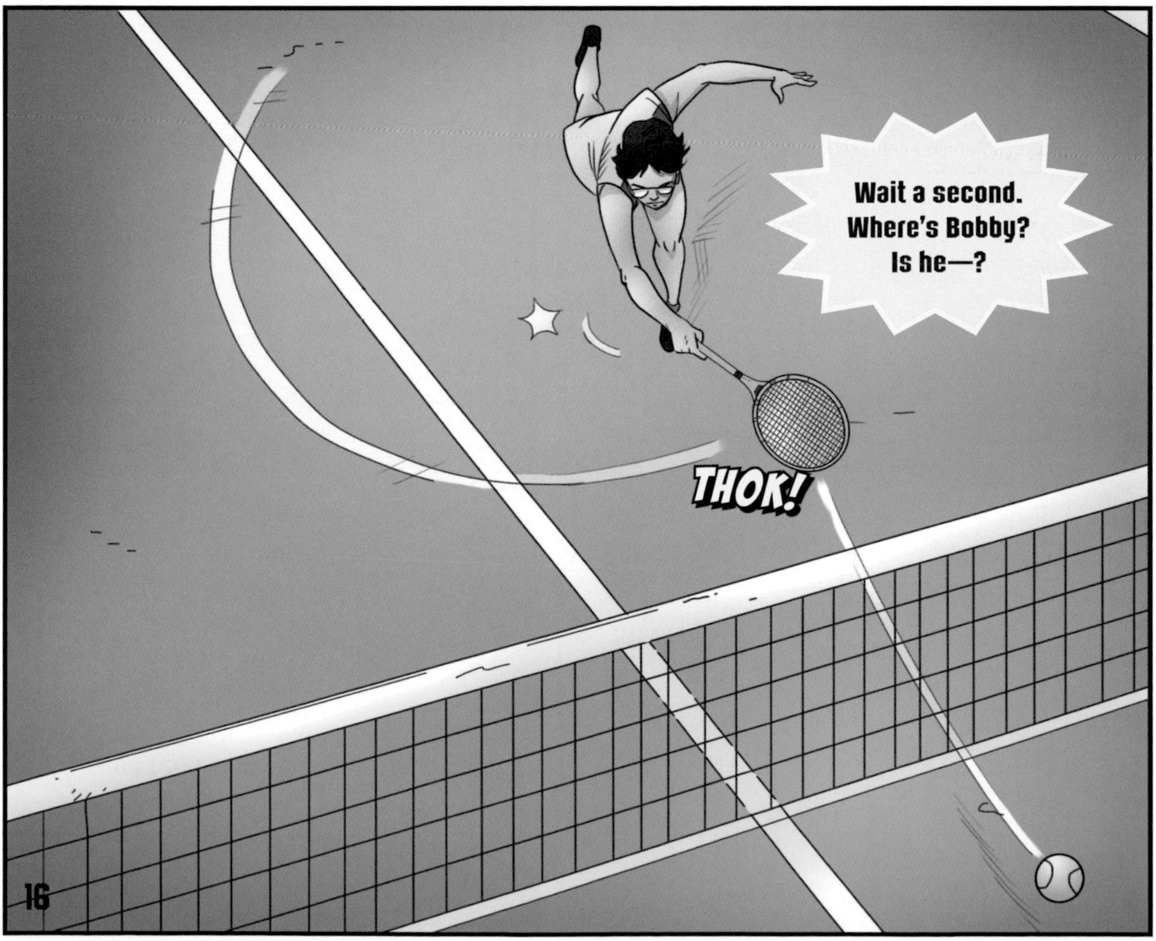
Wait a second. Where's Bobby? Is he—?
THOK!

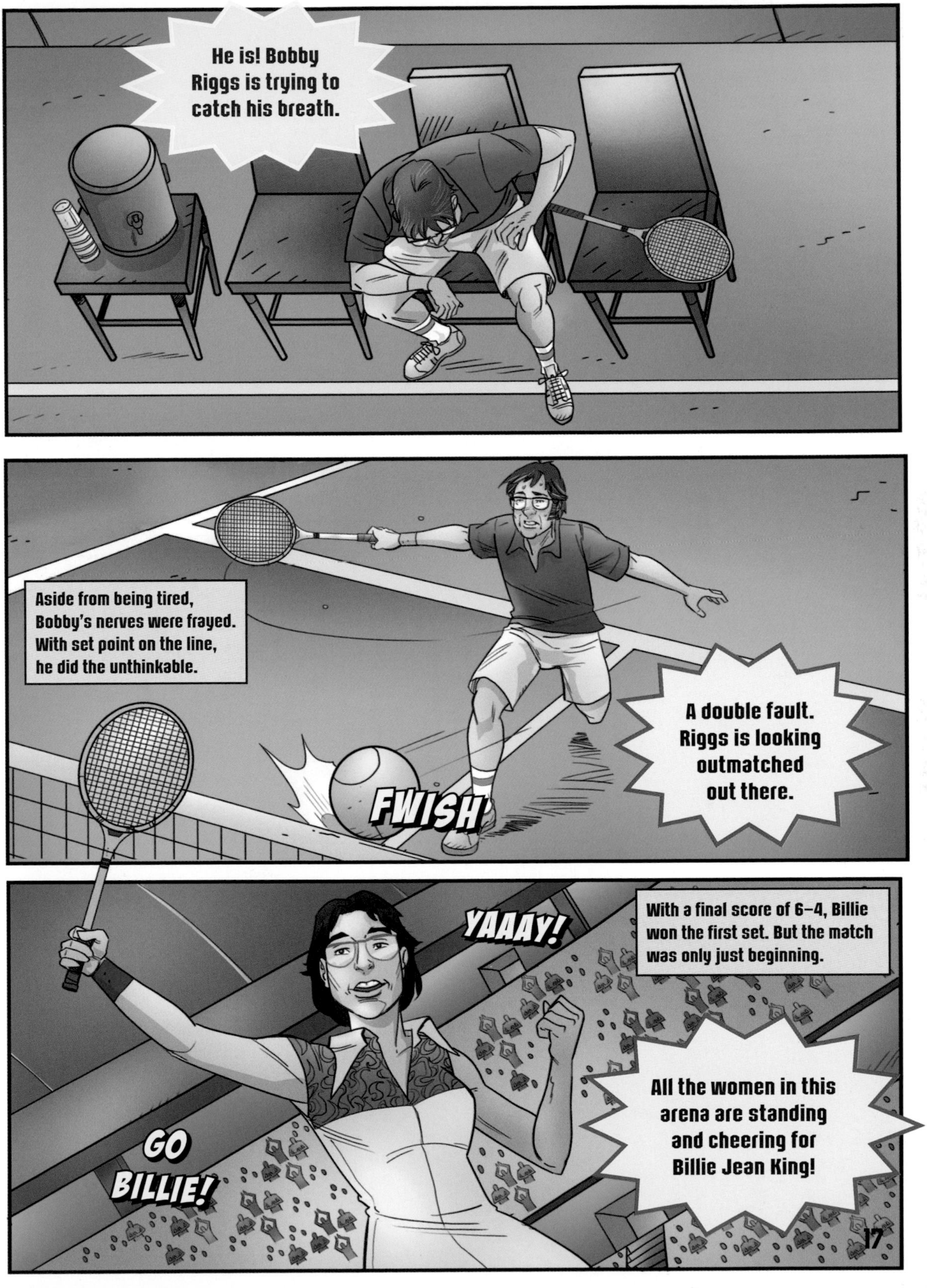
He is! Bobby Riggs is trying to catch his breath.
Aside from being tired, Bobby's nerves were frayed. With set point on the line, he did the unthinkable.
FWISH
A double fault. Riggs is looking outmatched out there.
YAAAY!
With a final score of 6–4, Billie won the first set. But the match was only just beginning.
All the women in this arena are standing and cheering for Billie Jean King!
GO BILLIE!

THE SECOND SET

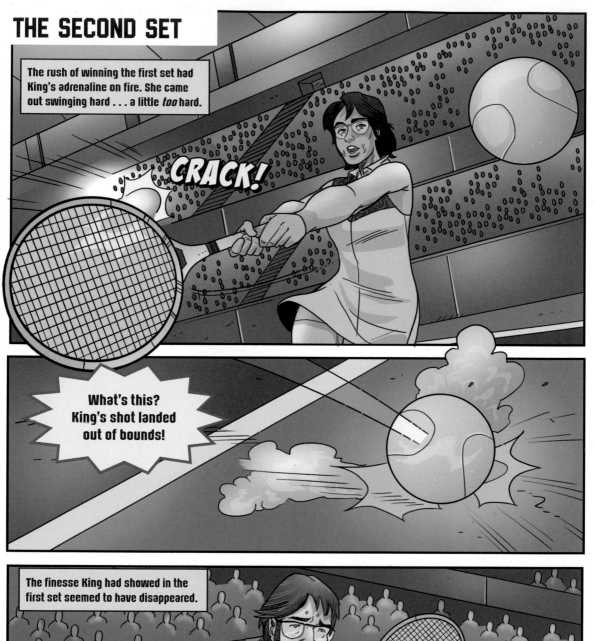

The rush of winning the first set had King's adrenaline on fire. She came out swinging hard . . . a little *too* hard.

CRACK!

What's this? King's shot landed out of bounds!

The finesse King had showed in the first set seemed to have disappeared.

A tired and out-of-shape Bobby Riggs saw a chance to possibly get back into the match.

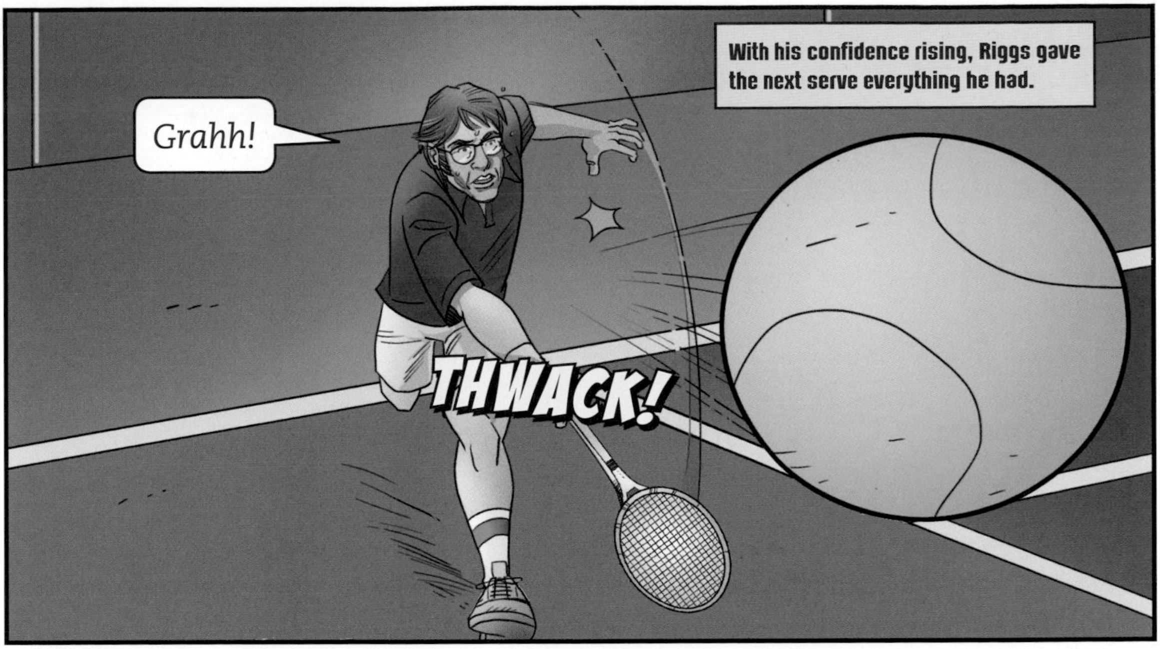
With his confidence rising, Riggs gave the next serve everything he had.
Grahh!
THWACK!

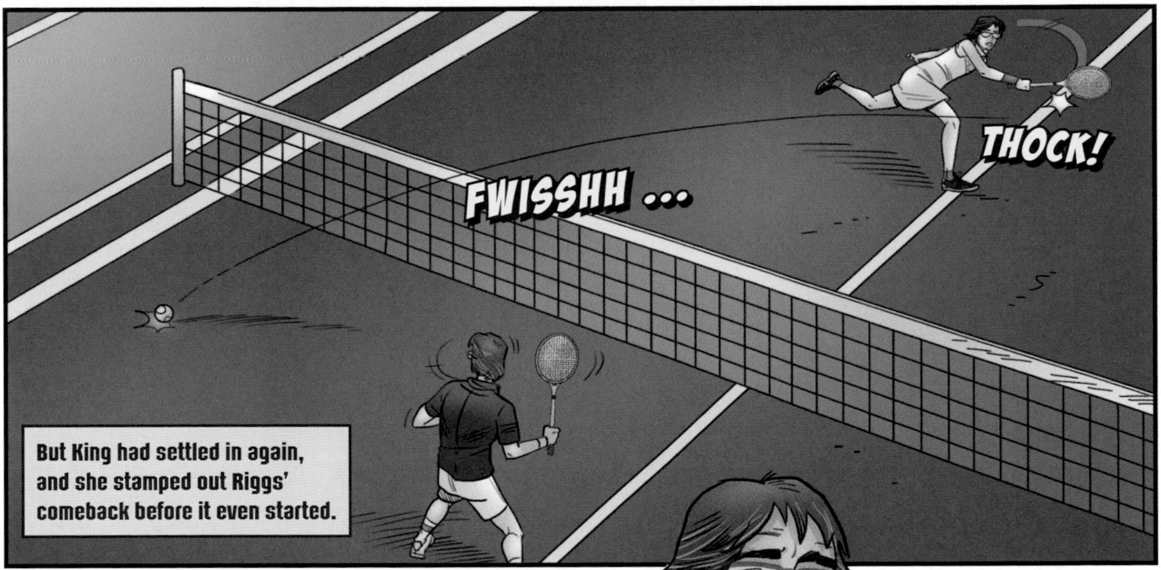
THOCK!
FWISSHH ...
But King had settled in again, and she stamped out Riggs' comeback before it even started.

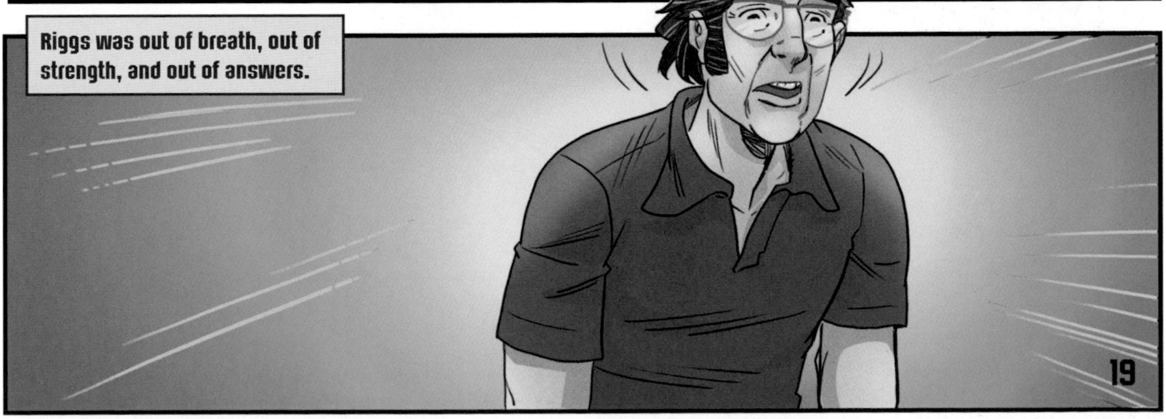
Riggs was out of breath, out of strength, and out of answers.

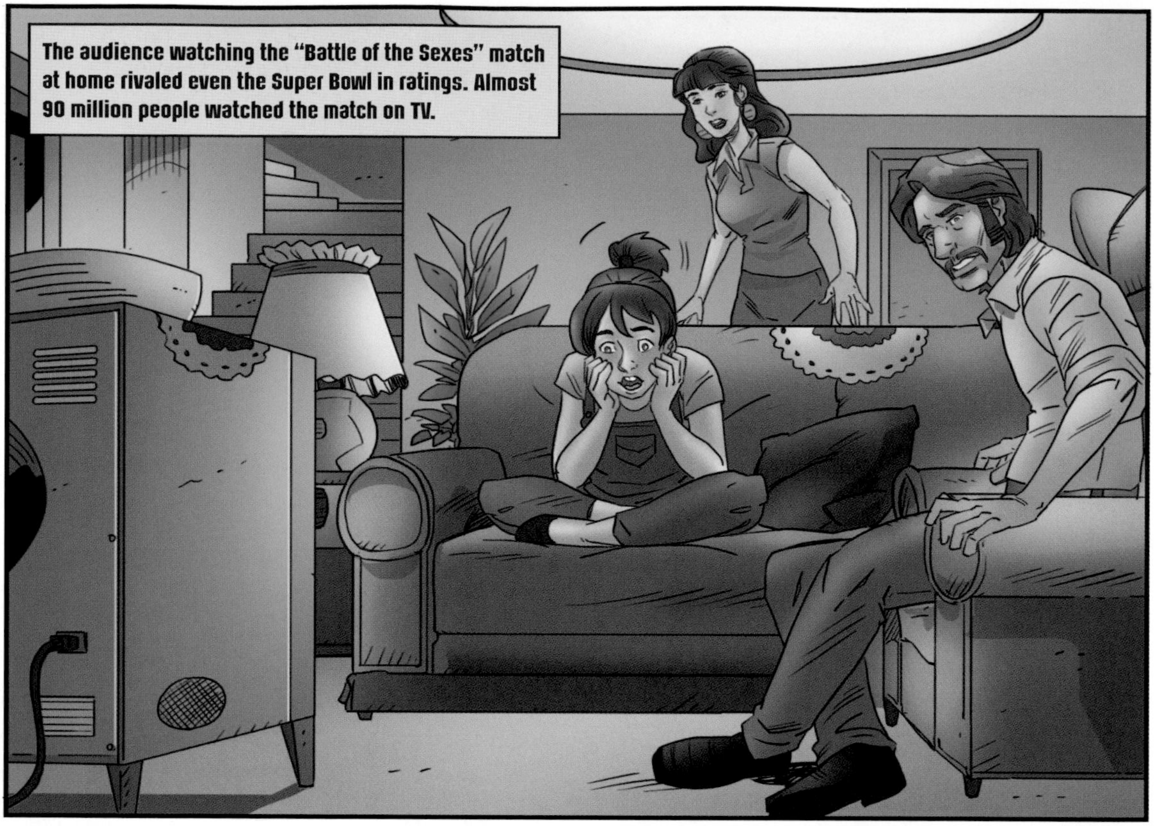
The audience watching the "Battle of the Sexes" match at home rivaled even the Super Bowl in ratings. Almost 90 million people watched the match on TV.

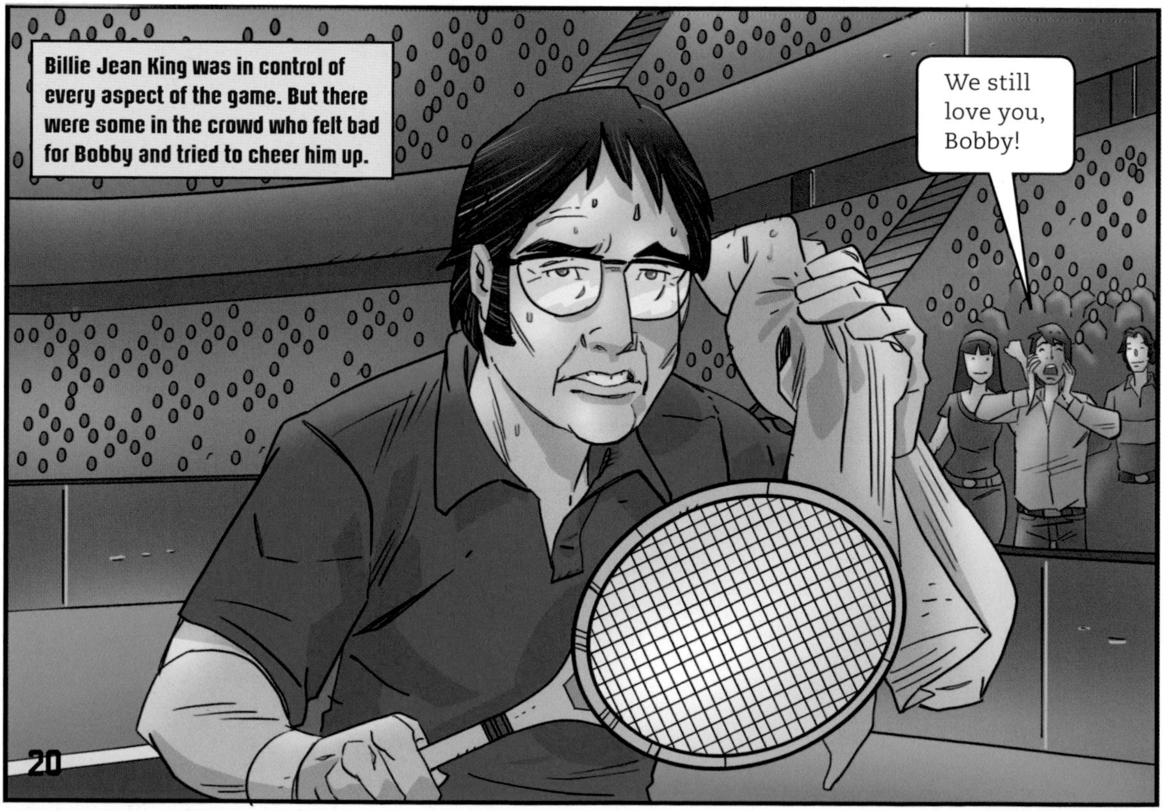
Billie Jean King was in control of every aspect of the game. But there were some in the crowd who felt bad for Bobby and tried to cheer him up.
We still love you, Bobby!

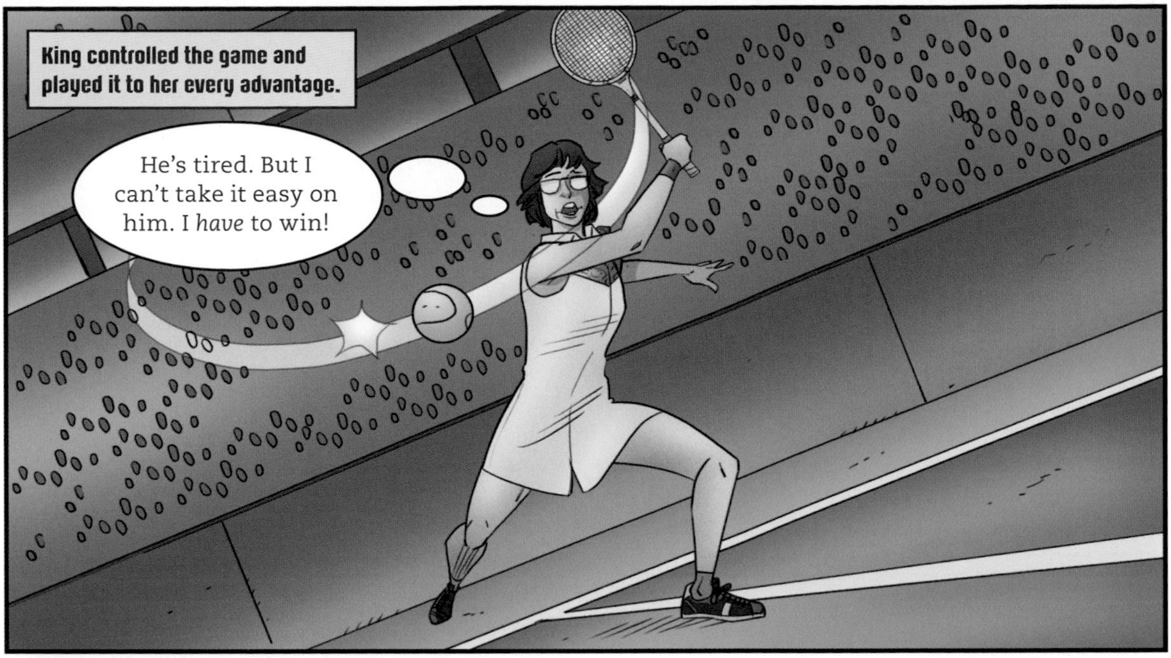
King controlled the game and played it to her every advantage.
He's tired. But I can't take it easy on him. I *have* to win!

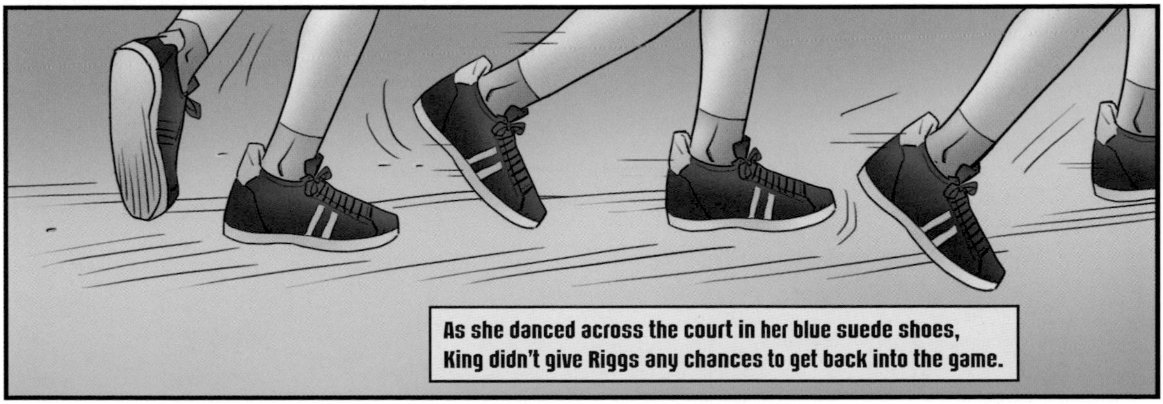
As she danced across the court in her blue suede shoes, King didn't give Riggs any chances to get back into the game.

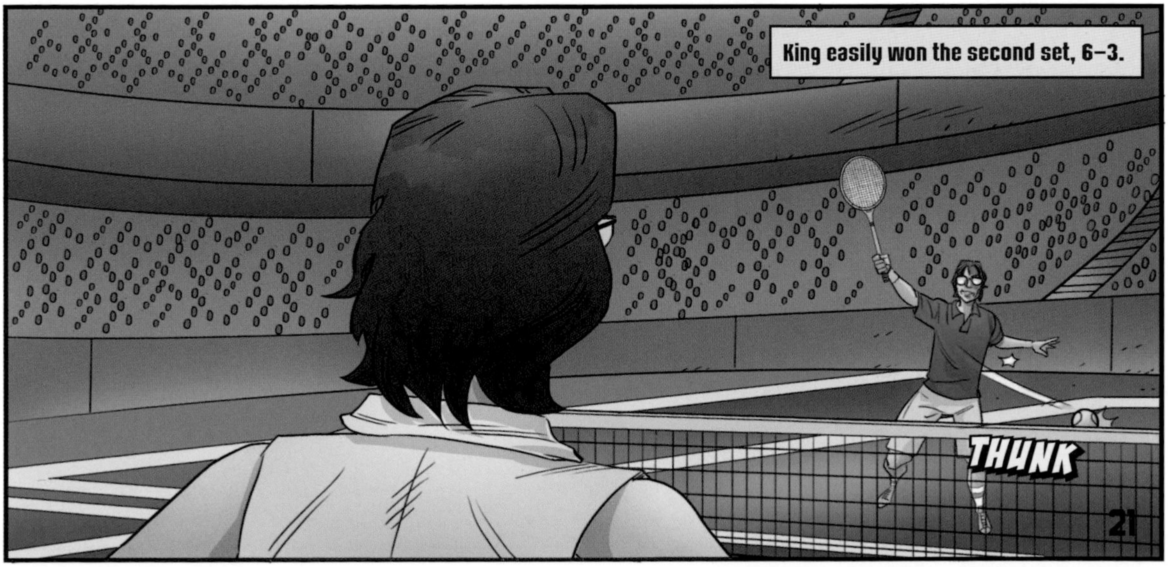
King easily won the second set, 6–3.
THUNK

VICTORY!

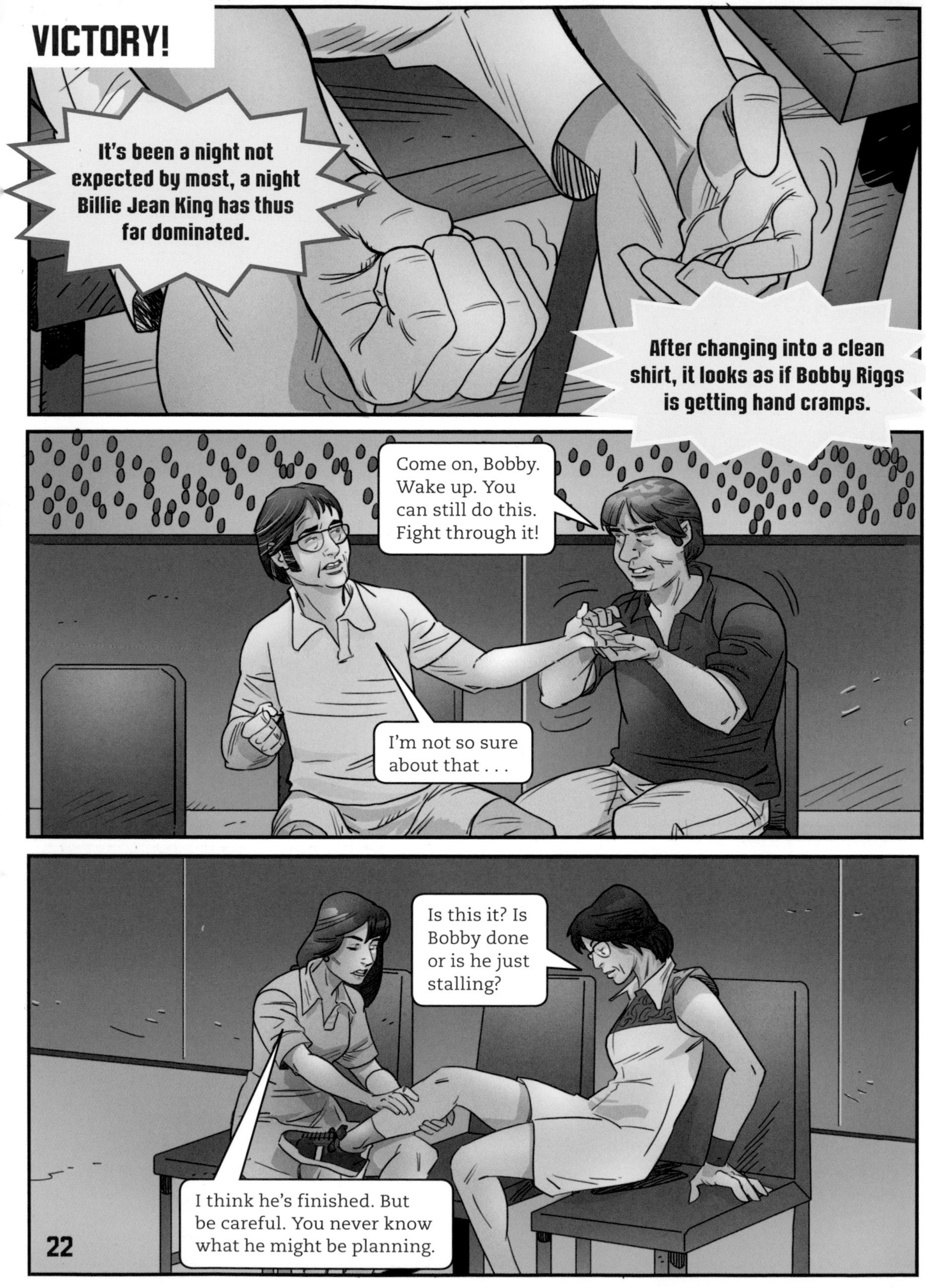

It's been a night not expected by most, a night Billie Jean King has thus far dominated.
After changing into a clean shirt, it looks as if Bobby Riggs is getting hand cramps.
Come on, Bobby. Wake up. You can still do this. Fight through it!
I'm not so sure about that . . .
Is this it? Is Bobby done or is he just stalling?
I think he's finished. But be careful. You never know what he might be planning.

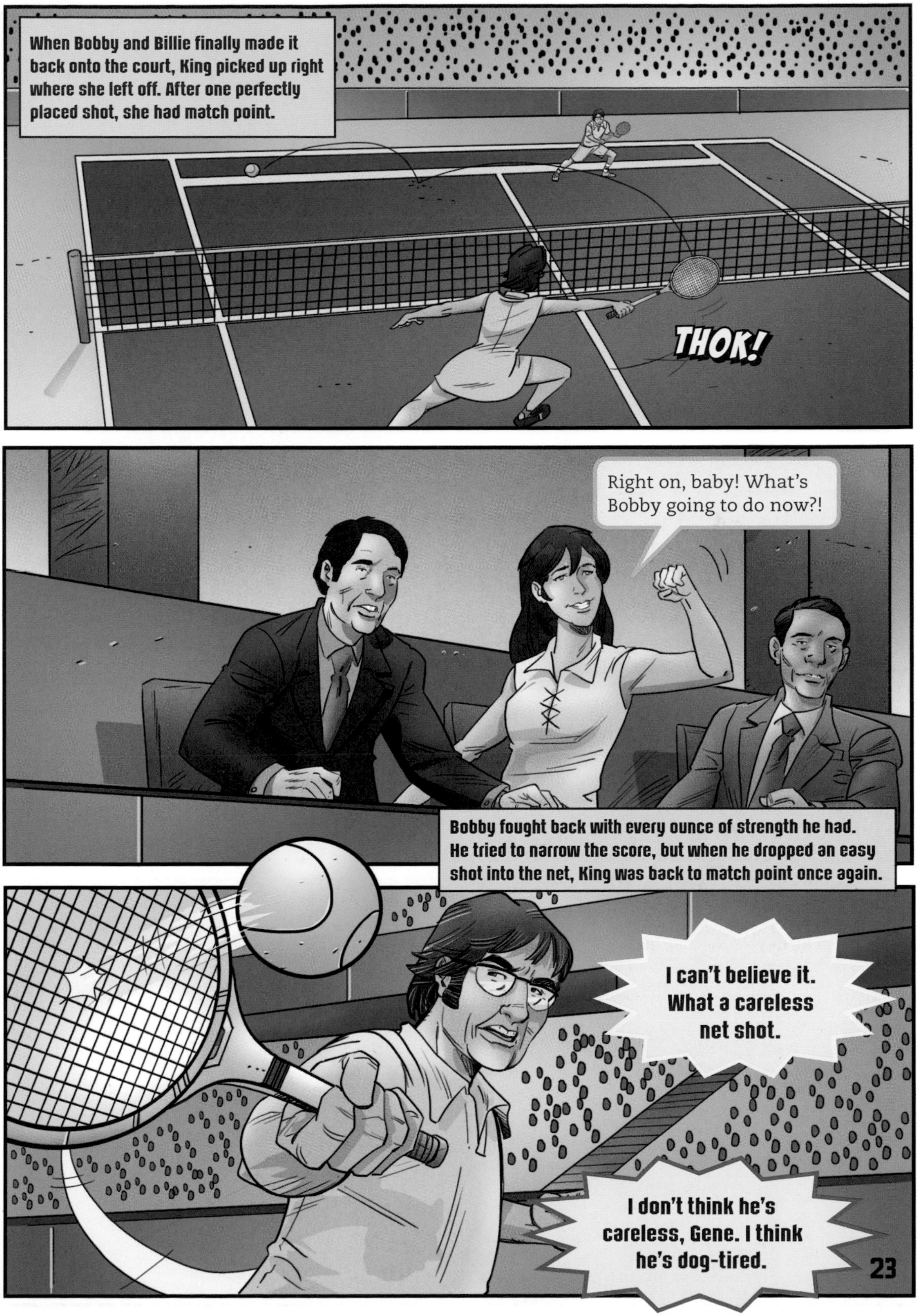

When Bobby and Billie finally made it back onto the court, King picked up right where she left off. After one perfectly placed shot, she had match point.
THOK!
Right on, baby! What's Bobby going to do now?!
Bobby fought back with every ounce of strength he had. He tried to narrow the score, but when he dropped an easy shot into the net, King was back to match point once again.
I can't believe it. What a careless net shot.
I don't think he's careless, Gene. I think he's dog-tired.

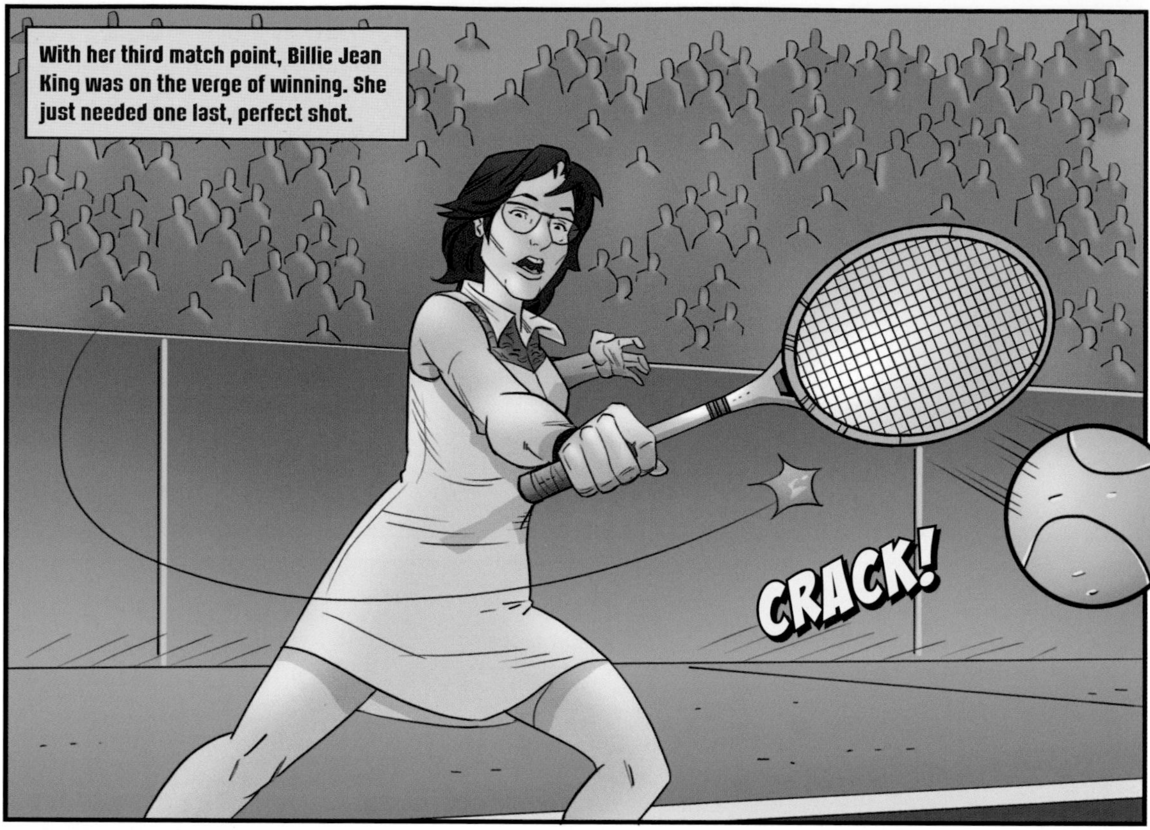
With her third match point, Billie Jean King was on the verge of winning. She just needed one last, perfect shot.
CRACK!

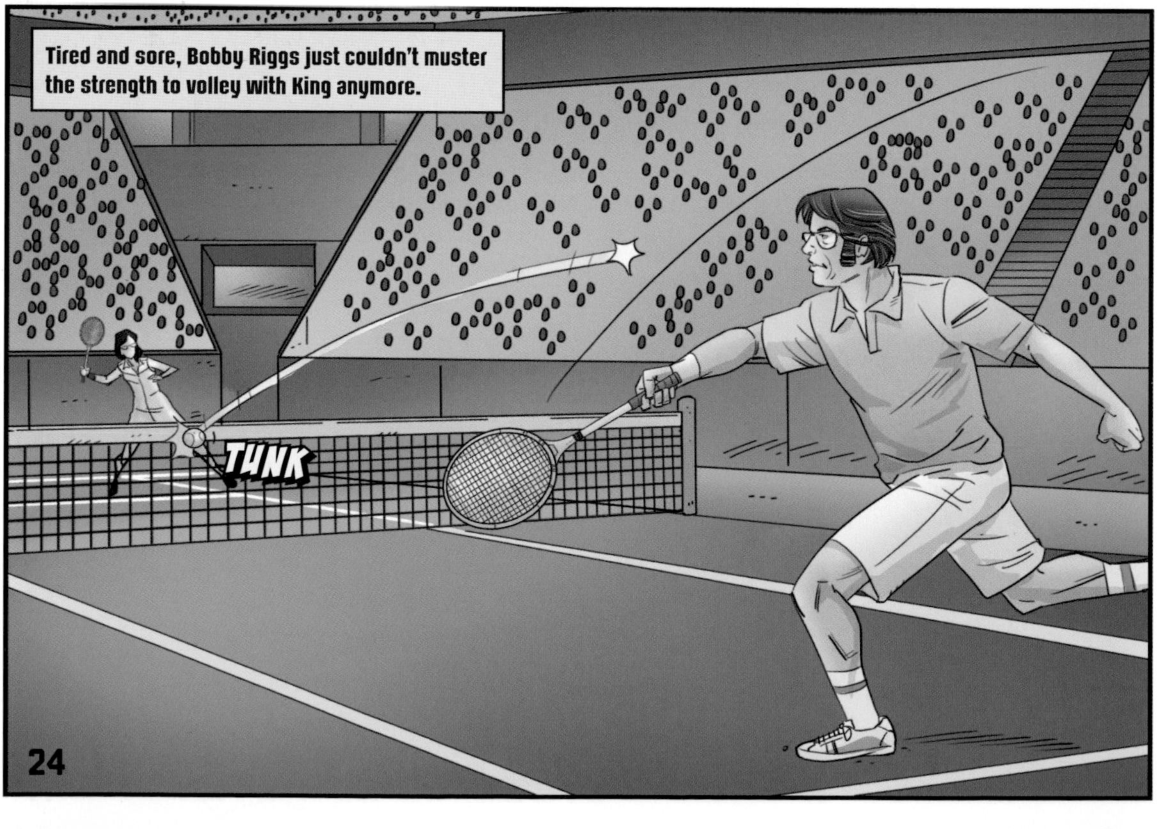
Tired and sore, Bobby Riggs just couldn't muster the strength to volley with King anymore.
TUNK

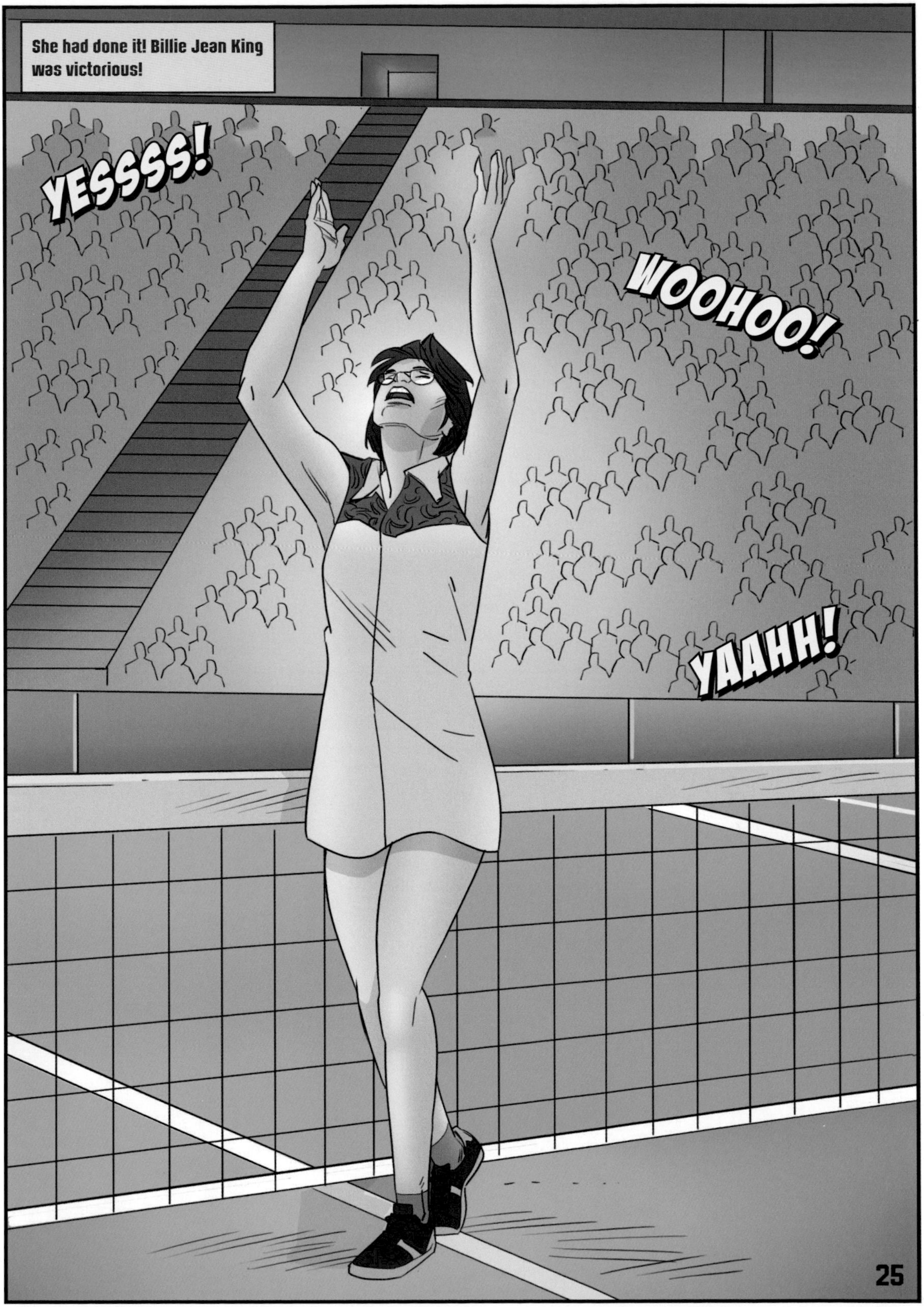

She had done it! Billie Jean King was victorious!
YESSSS!
WOOHOO!
YAAHH!

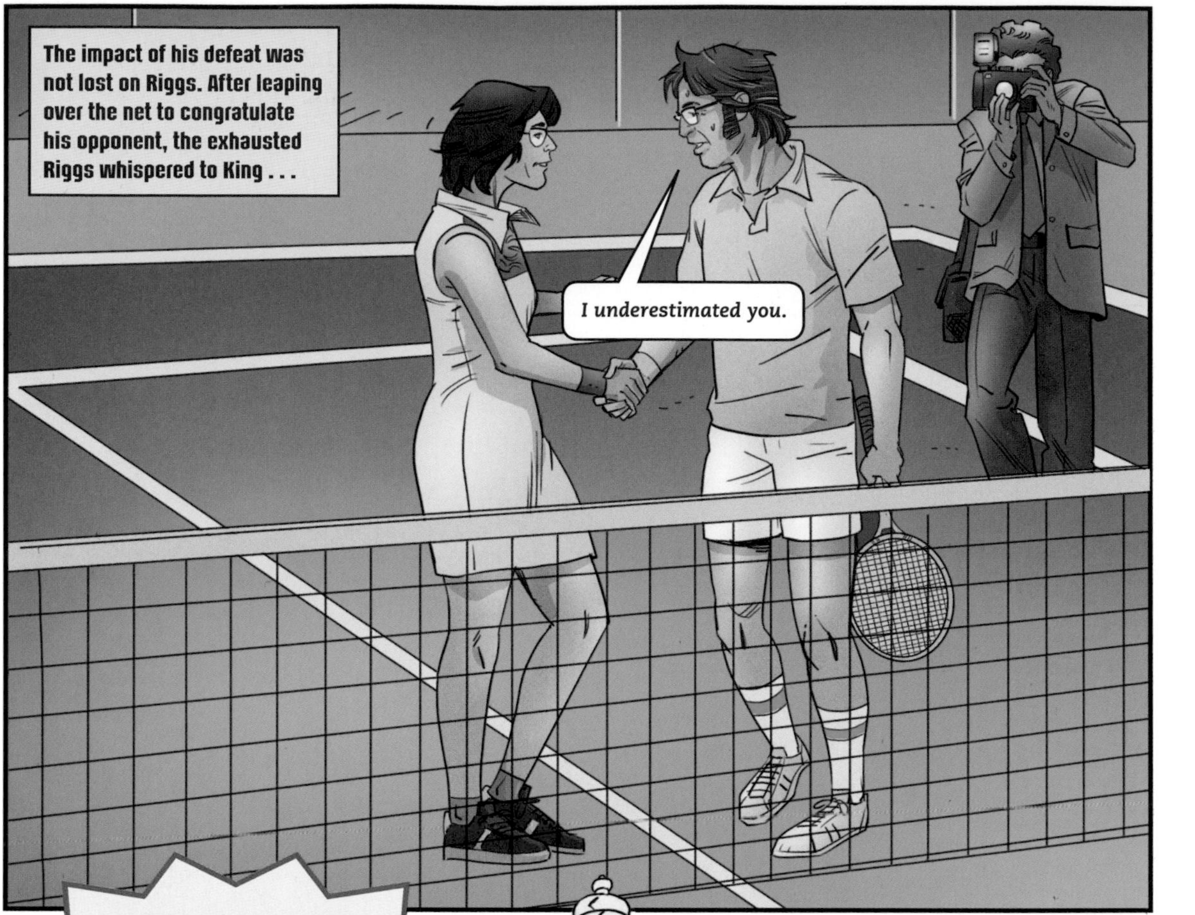
The impact of his defeat was not lost on Riggs. After leaping over the net to congratulate his opponent, the exhausted Riggs whispered to King . . .
I underestimated you.

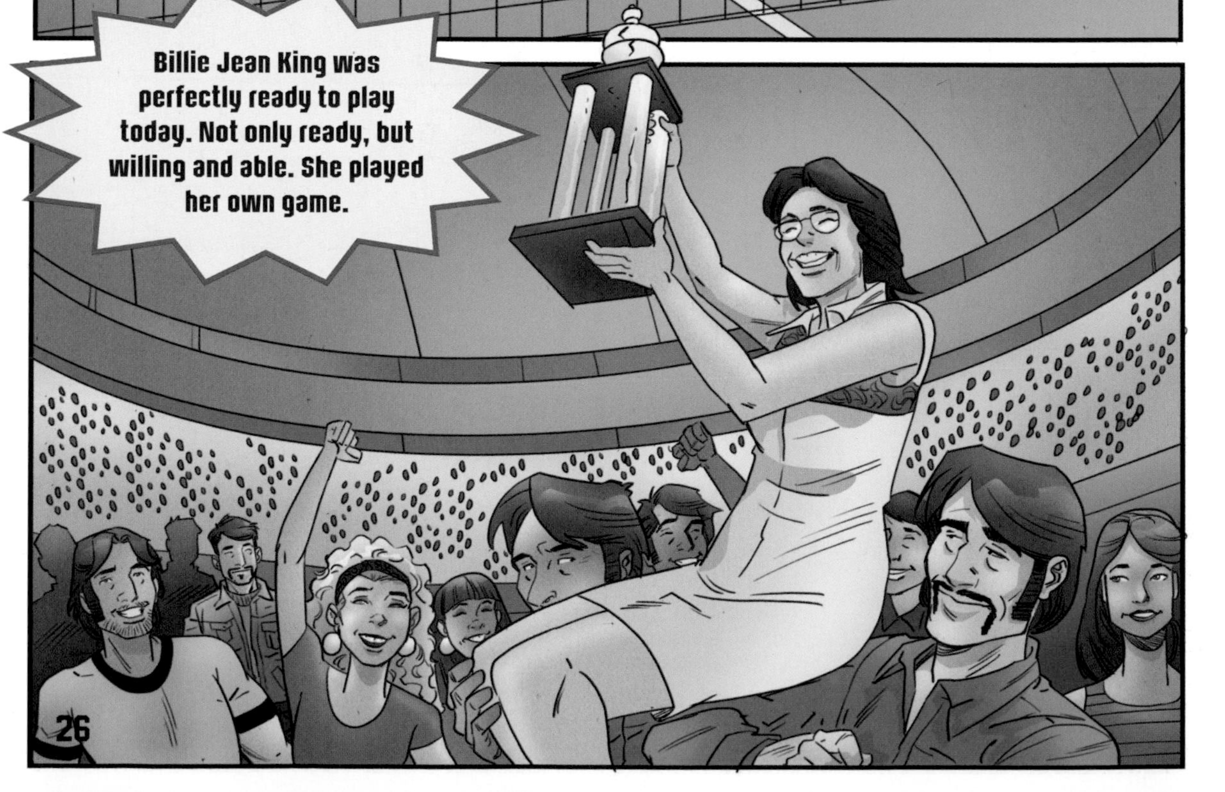
Billie Jean King was perfectly ready to play today. Not only ready, but willing and able. She played her own game.

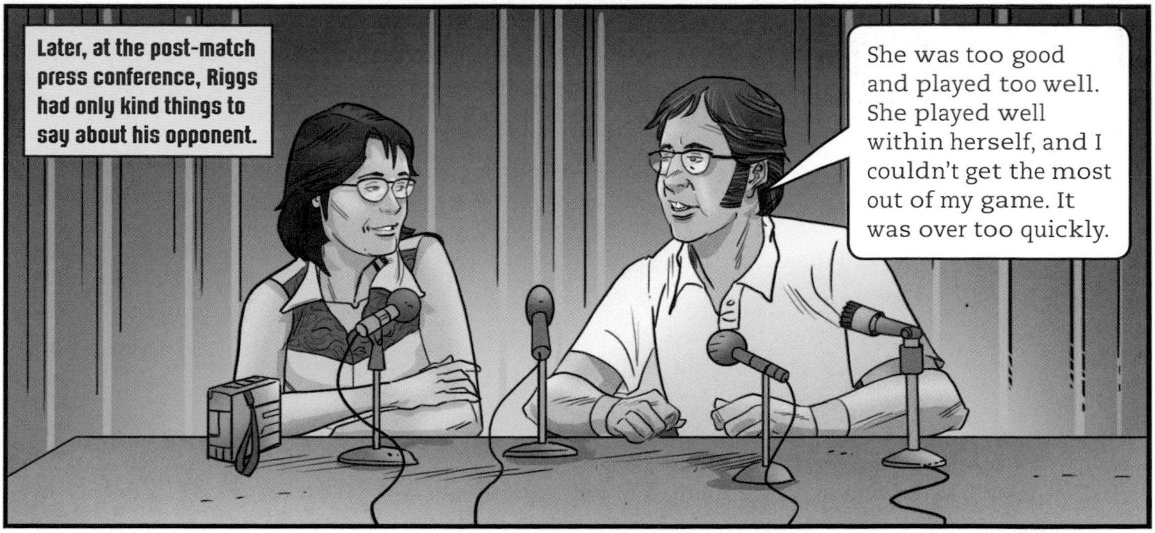
Later, at the post-match press conference, Riggs had only kind things to say about his opponent.
She was too good and played too well. She played well within herself, and I couldn't get the most out of my game. It was over too quickly.

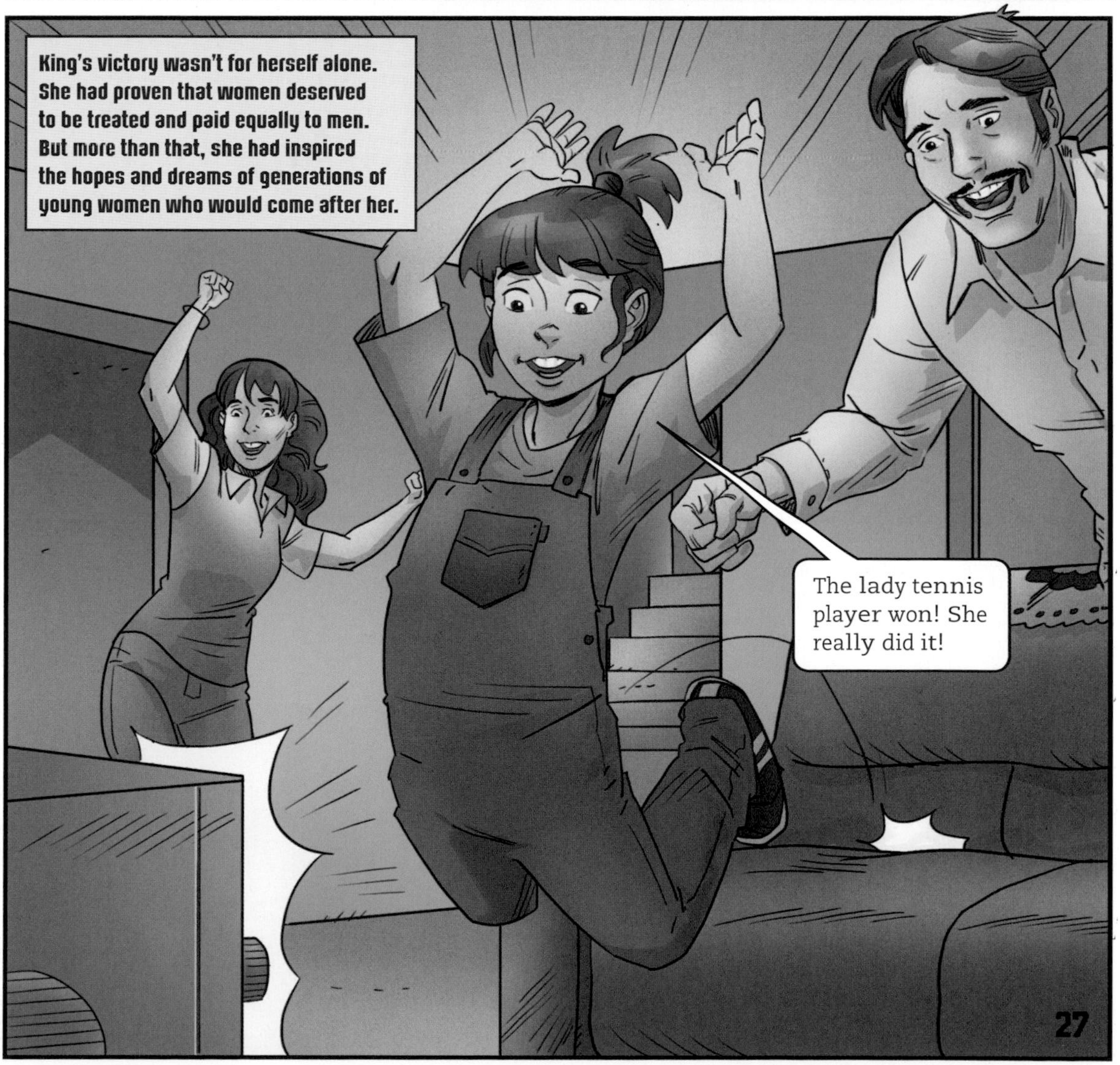
King's victory wasn't for herself alone. She had proven that women deserved to be treated and paid equally to men. But more than that, she had inspired the hopes and dreams of generations of young women who would come after her.
The lady tennis player won! She really did it!

LASTING LEGACIES

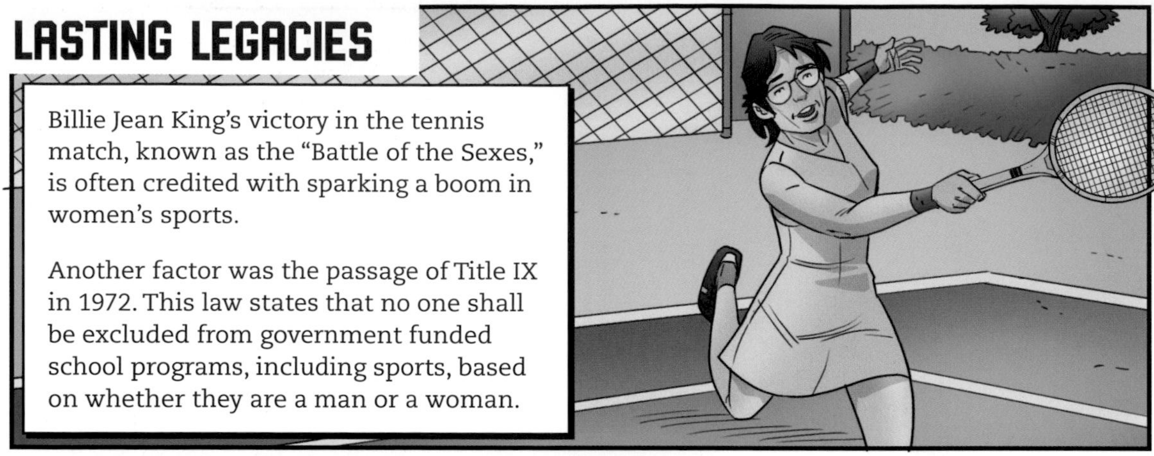

Billie Jean King's victory in the tennis match, known as the "Battle of the Sexes," is often credited with sparking a boom in women's sports.
Another factor was the passage of Title IX in 1972. This law states that no one shall be excluded from government funded school programs, including sports, based on whether they are a man or a woman.

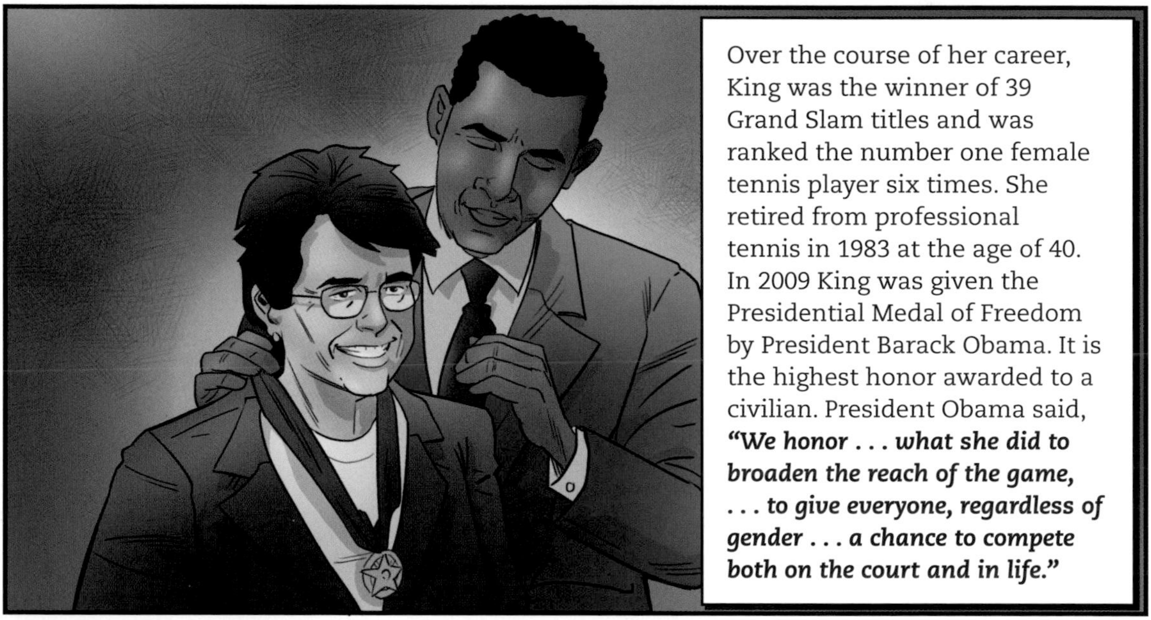

Over the course of her career, King was the winner of 39 Grand Slam titles and was ranked the number one female tennis player six times. She retired from professional tennis in 1983 at the age of 40. In 2009 King was given the Presidential Medal of Freedom by President Barack Obama. It is the highest honor awarded to a civilian. President Obama said, ***"We honor . . . what she did to broaden the reach of the game, . . . to give everyone, regardless of gender . . . a chance to compete both on the court and in life."***

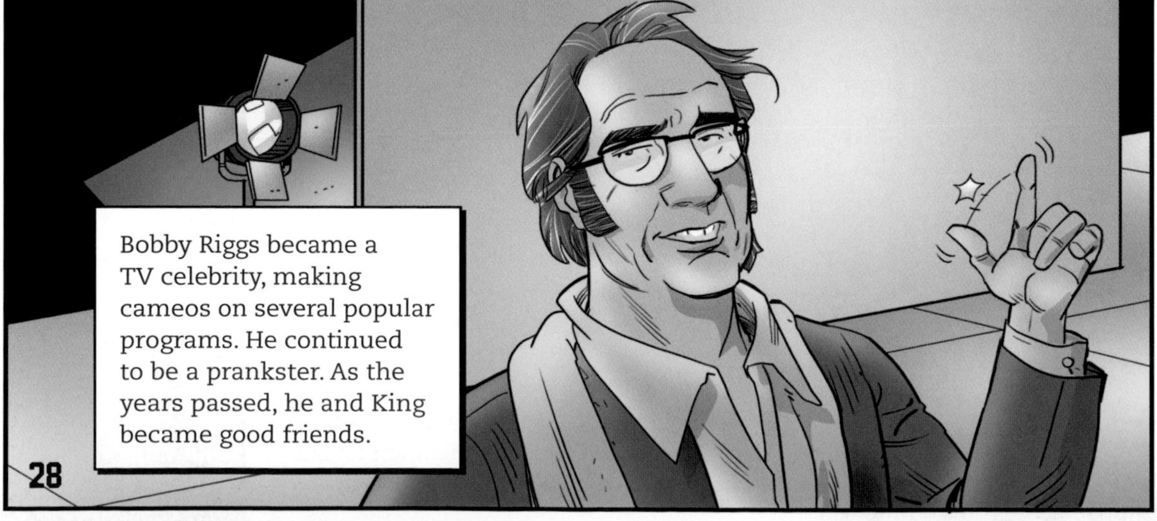

Bobby Riggs became a TV celebrity, making cameos on several popular programs. He continued to be a prankster. As the years passed, he and King became good friends.

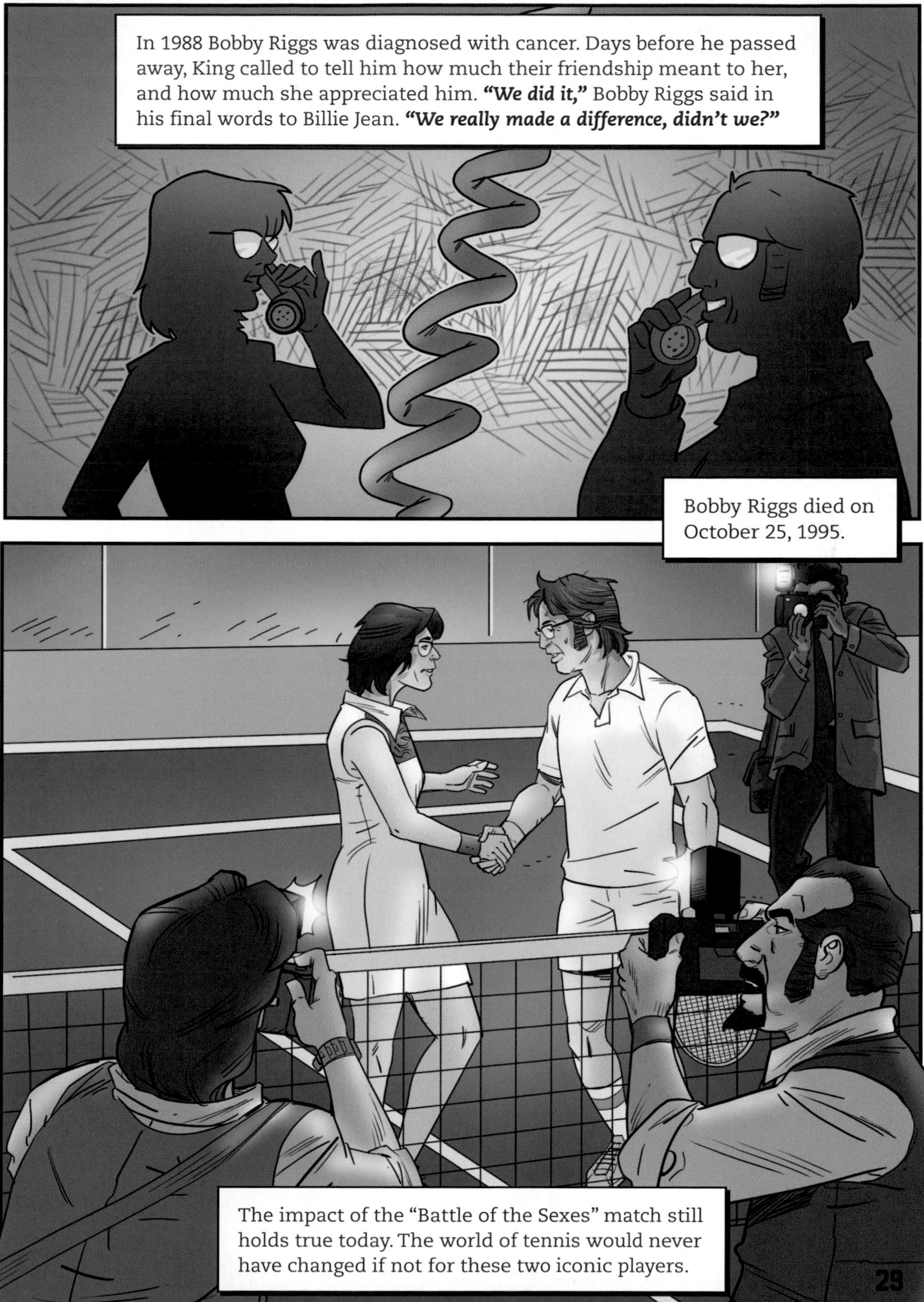
In 1988 Bobby Riggs was diagnosed with cancer. Days before he passed away, King called to tell him how much their friendship meant to her, and how much she appreciated him. ***"We did it,"*** Bobby Riggs said in his final words to Billie Jean. ***"We really made a difference, didn't we?"***
Bobby Riggs died on October 25, 1995.
The impact of the "Battle of the Sexes" match still holds true today. The world of tennis would never have changed if not for these two iconic players.

GLOSSARY

adrenaline (uh-DREH-nuh-luhn)—a chemical the body produces when a person is excited

advantage (ad-VAN-tij)—something that is helpful or useful

diagnose (dy-ig-NOHS)—to find the cause of a problem

fault (FAWLT)—a tennis serve that fails to land in the correct area of play

feminine (FEM-uh-nuhn)—having qualities typically associated with women

finesse (fih-NESS)—skillful handling of a difficult situation

match point (MACH POINT)—when a player needs just one more point to win a match

rickshaw (RIK-shaw)—a small carriage that is usually pulled by a person

rivalry (RYE-val-ree)—a fierce feeling of competition between two people

set (SET)—a unit of scoring games; the first player to win six games with a two-game advantage wins the set

volley (VOL-ee)—a shot made by hitting the ball over the net before it bounces

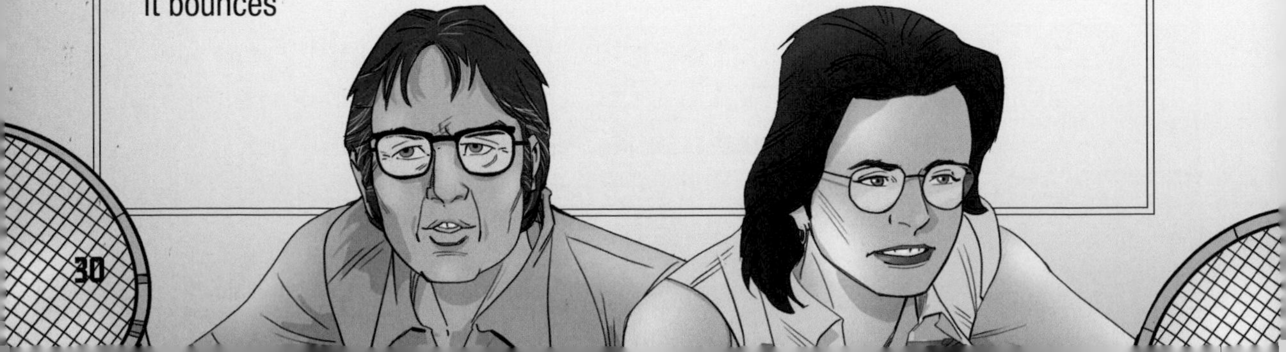

READ MORE

Gitlin, Marty. *The Best Tennis Players of All Time.* Sports' Best Ever. Minneapolis: ABDO Publishing, 2015.

Monnig, Alex. *Serena Williams vs. Billie Jean King.* Versus. Minneapolis: ABDO Publishing, 2018.

Skinner, J. E. *Billie Jean King vs. Bobby Riggs.* Sports Unite Us. Ann Arbor, Mich.: Cherry Lake Publishing, 2018.

CRITICAL THINKING QUESTIONS

- Billie Jean King spent the majority of her career fighting for women's equality in professional tennis. How do you think this affected her life, both on and off the court?

- Think about the different ways Billie Jean King and Bobby Riggs behaved in the story. What lessons can young athletes learn about good sportsmanship and how to treat others?

- Imagine you're a child watching the famous tennis match as it happened on TV. Write about what you think it was like to see a woman defeat a man for the first time.

INTERNET SITES

Use Facthound to find Internet sites related to this book.

Visit *www.facthound.com*

Just type in 9781543542196 and go.

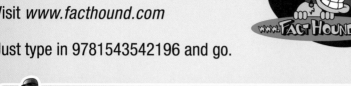

Super-cool stuff!

Check out projects, games and lots more at
www.capstonekids.com

INDEX